The Laws of Perseverance

~ Reversing Your Common Sense ~

RYUHO OKAWA
FOUNDER OF HAPPY SCIENCE

Second Edition, with 2022 updates
Copyright © 2014 by Ryuho Okawa
English translation © Happy Science 2014
Original title: "Nintai-no-Hō"
All rights reserved
HS Press is an imprint of IRH Press Co., Ltd.
Tokyo
ISBN 13: 979-8-88737-043-9

Contents

2

Triumphing Over Trials
~ How to Live Your Life with No Regrets ~

⌒○   # 3   ○⌒

Generating Virtue
~ Become Selfless and Live for Your Calling ~

4

The Undefeated

~ How to Live Beyond the Wins and Losses of This World ~

3. Shakyamuni Buddha's Renunciation and the Destruction of His Homeland

4. Why Unreasonable Incidents Happen in This World

5. Endure Not Being Approved Of

6. Messengers of God Who Died for the Truth

7. People Who Live in the Truth Are Undefeatable

5

The Reversal of Your Common Sense
~ The Power of Truth That Will Open Up the New Era ~

1. The Battle Against the Common Sense of the Times

2. The Common Sense of the Religious World Tramples on God's Heart

Postscript 235

Preface

A religious leader, as a vocation, is indeed one that puts himself through a rigorous training. Strengthening the power to persevere, in particular, is an inevitable discipline.

To start with, we must endure opposition from our parents, siblings, spouses and relatives, then gossip and insults from neighbors and colleagues, complaints from customers, and spiteful criticism from tabloids.

Furthermore, we must endure against the major newspapers and TV channels that exercise their right to continually neglect and ignore our efforts, no matter how hard we try. Sometimes we must also withstand oppression by the government and bureaucrats.

Also, while a religious organization develops, there will always be people in that group whose mission comes to an end. There is a need to endure against such people from holding back competent disciples who came later and obstructing the organization from the outside.

On the whole, to protect the light of Truth forever, we must keep on fighting against the common sense of society, academics and traditional religions. The extreme examples of greats in history, in these pages, shall always lift your soul.

December 10, 2013
Master & CEO of Happy Science Group
Ryuho Okawa

No Matter the Pain

No matter the pain,
Do not complain.
Life is not always an effortless walk.

Climbing a hill
Is painful to all.
A time for patience
Will certainly come.

A coil spring that stretches well
Also compresses well.
You must store energy first
Before you expand.

It is sad

To see the leaves fall

In autumn,

But that is not the end.

Though it may seem like all are lost,

The buds for next spring

Are silently lying in wait.

Thorough preparations are in progress

By the life unseen.

So,

No matter the pain,

Do not complain.

Continue to store your energy

For the next chance to leap.

CHAPTER ONE

How to Overcome Slumps

~ For Those Who Wish to Improve Their Fortune ~

Lecture given on May 8, 2002
at Happy Science General Headquarters
Tokyo, Japan

1. Everyone Experiences Slumps

Slumps occur in various situations

The theme of this chapter is how to overcome slumps. A slump is, by definition, a decline or a period of poor performance. Generally speaking, we use the expression "fall into a slump" when something that had been going fairly well abruptly falls apart.

If we use the word slump in connection to children or students, it could refer to a time when an honor-roll student suddenly falls behind or an athletic student suddenly starts performing poorly. For example, there are times when the cleanup hitter (usually one of the best hitters) in a high school baseball team just cannot seem to hit the ball. A player who boasted a high batting average in the regional tournament may become so nervous in the national tournament that he keeps missing the ball and cannot get a clean hit. In the world of sports, times like this are often called slumps.

Slumps can also occur at work. If you work for a company, there are periods when suddenly you can do nothing right. Everyone may have experienced times when, all of a sudden, things do not go smoothly, although everything was going well up until then. Of course, it may not be considered a slump if the economy is declining, and if companies and people everywhere are also in poor shape.

In contrast, there are times when you alone are performing poorly, even though your surroundings have not changed. For example, your sales plummet and you cannot come up with any ideas in project meetings, or even if you do, they are flops. When you were on a roll, all of your ideas yielded best selling products, but sometimes this ceases to happen.

Slumps can also occur in personal relationships. There are cases where a good relationship is soured after you make some kind of false step. Then, all of a sudden, you find yourself falling out with your other friends, too, and you end up being isolated. There are times when personal relationships go sour and you lose your confidence in everything. Of course, there may be other elements involved if you look at the big picture.

Slumps occur not only for individuals but for particular groups, too. In baseball, for instance, there are times when the whole team's performance drops, and in companies, there are times when an entire organization starts doing poorly. An organization that embraces, to some degree, the same values or attitudes, can sometimes go into a collective slump. But in this chapter, I would like to focus on personal slumps.

Cycles of fortune are accepted as an empirical law

The words luck and fortune are familiar, and from ancient times it has been widely known that there are "waves of fortune" or "waves of luck" in life. There are times when your luck gets better and you start doing extremely well, and times when your luck worsens and your performance drops. For this reason, different kinds of fortune telling, such as theories explaining that those waves happen in cycles of 12 years, have become popular.

In recent years, cycles known as biorhythms have been used when selling life insurance. Many of you may have experienced a sales pitch like, "People experience waves called biorhythms based on their date of birth. Looking at your birth date and other elements such as your horoscope, your luck will be this way."

Unlike normal kinds of fortune telling, biorhythms are related to physiological or bodily conditions, so sometimes you can see why you are low on energy by looking at these waves. Of course, the wave cycles are different depending on the individual, but in one sense, you can prepare yourself somewhat by having a good understanding of these waves.

However, if your mind sticks to this kind of idea or you develop strong preconceived notions, it can be harmful. For example, if you are told, "You are currently on the wave leading into a slump," then you will be influenced by this sort of suggestion and it will most likely bring about an actual slump. Those who tend to be quick to believe in fortune telling are susceptible to negative suggestion, so they must be careful not to let this happen.

In the long span of history, people have understood, as an empirical law, that these kinds of cycles or waves of fortune exist. It is rather difficult to create a definite theory out of this or to explain them precisely. If these waves could be understood precisely, people could make flourishing businesses using them. In fact, these waves are still quite a mystery, so people generally cannot make use of them to expand their businesses.

In any case, here I would like to focus on the general theme of slumps and talk about what you should bear in mind, how you should conduct yourself and how to lead your life at such times.

2. What to Be Aware of When You Are in a Slump

Outstanding people tend to fall into a slump

Among my readers, some may say that they have never experienced a slump. Of course, it is truly wonderful if there are people who are always in top-notch condition and constantly doing well. I really appreciate such people and I'm sure that others can do nothing but applaud them as well.

However, I have to say that in many cases, those who have never experienced a slump often lead a very mundane life, so there is no way that they will fall into one. In that sense, it is not necessarily good never to have experienced slumps.

Someone who barely studies, exercises or works properly, who pays no heed to personal relationships and simply lives his or her life like a jellyfish drifting aimlessly in the ocean, may never experience a real slump. So, if this is the case, please do not misunderstand me.

After all, a slump is when people who normally perform better than others or are admired for their abilities or work, experience a sudden decline in performance. This is when they feel that they have fallen into a slump.

In baseball, for example, if a batter only hits 10% of the balls from the very start and says that he is "in a slump," it's not actually a slump but merely a lack of talent. No matter how much he bemoans, "What's happening? I must be in a slump. I just can't hit the ball," the fact is that he did not have the ability to hit the ball in the first place. It is only considered a slump if a batter who usually hits 30% or 40% of the balls can no longer hit them, so please do not be confused about this point. If there is a fundamental problem with your basic ability, you must practice and improve your skills rather than complain that you're in a slump.

A slump is when someone with a certain degree of ability, who normally carries out his or her work energetically, starts performing poorly. Slumps also happen to the type of people who are always chasing after lofty ideals and who expect a great deal of themselves. They occur to those perfectionists who are satisfied with themselves only when they get full marks in their studies, sports and work.

In that sense, Happy Science members must be careful because many of them are idealists in search of ideals. They may feel very disappointed with themselves when they cannot do their absolute best. There are certainly various causes for a slump so in many cases, they may suffer, thinking, "Although everything was going smoothly, things suddenly stopped going well from the start of this year."

Thus, many people may suffer slumps, but I want you to understand that you fall into a slump because you are an outstanding person in some respect. Please be aware of this first.

You must possess something out of the ordinary, some excellence, something that other people do not have, be it your talent, your ability to perform, your aspiration or your ideals. Or perhaps you are making an effort to become like that. That is why you experience slumps.

Tragedies that happen to people because they are elite

When things are not going well, people tend to reject themselves, feeling that they are no good, and become dissatisfied with everything they do. They sometimes drive themselves into a corner, become depressed and even go as far as committing suicide.

This can often happen to the most talented, most able people. Actually, it is because they feel they are superior that when they can see no way forward, they kill themselves. This is a matter of mindset, so you must be careful.

It seems that nowadays many of the people who commit suicide belong to the elite. The academic or business elite are usually on the fast track. When they lose out to colleagues of their own age, get demoted or encounter some kind of difficulty, they suddenly fall into despair and choose to put an end to their lives.

In Japan, suicides often occur at workplaces where exclusive elites gather, compared to the overall average of Japanese people. For example, I have heard that at a certain government office, 10% of new recruits commit suicide. In some ways, people who are said to be "talented" from a worldly perspective easily become discouraged and choose to die.

The reason for their suicide may seem trivial to the world at large. In fact, they consider success and failure within the confines of a small group. It is as if they are competing to reach the summit of Mount Fuji from the 8th station, stressing over who is winning. Most people do not even reach the 8th station; usually, people give up somewhere between the 3rd and 5th station. However, those ten or twenty people who have reached the cloud-covered 8th station vie to reach the summit, and if they are overtaken, say things like, "He's faster than me. I can't bear losing so I'm going to end my life here." Such tragedies are very common. They are quick thinkers and see the outcome too swiftly. So, upon seeing that they will lose, they decide to end their lives prematurely.

They cannot get through such tough times solely with the ability to get high scores on exams; they need the power of religion. They must become stronger and endure such tough times. Otherwise there would be no reason for them to be born into this world. It is really sad that they judge their entire life based only on the results of competition within a limited world.

It also happens that people who are successful in their main occupation find it very hard to withstand other failures. They get depressed over matters that other people would see as common occurrences. For example, there are various kinds of relationship issues, such as problems with friends, parents, spouses, children or neighbors. Sometimes people have trouble with such relationships, and agonize over matters that would seem trivial to other people. As a result, this can affect their main occupation and even ruin what they have accomplished there. This often happens so you need to be careful about that.

Of course, people who are in a slump may see themselves as being in a pathetic state when compared with their past glory or their ideal selves. I can more than sympathize with that feeling. However, as the first point, please recognize and accept the fact that people who experience slumps are the ones with great character.

3. Think About How You Rank Overall

Look at yourself from a statistical point of view

People who are in a slump tend to put themselves down. It's because they are just comparing themselves to when they were at their best or their ideal selves. If they were to compare themselves with the whole of humankind or all people in their country, or with all men or all women, they would see that they are not completely hopeless or a waste of space.

There is no one anywhere who can judge them as no good. They might think of themselves as "the worst of men," "the worst of women," or "the greatest loser in the history of humankind." However, nobody can investigate such a thing. For example, a man may feel crushed when he is fully scolded at work by his boss and told, "This work is no good. It's just a load of rubbish!" or when the woman he loves turns him down. He may think that he is the most pathetic person who has ever lived and absolutely hopeless.

At such times, please think about yourself from a statistical point of view. That will show just how incorrectly you are judging yourself. If, within a limited world or social group, you find yourself thinking that you are "a loser," "the absolute worst," or "a hopeless human being," widen your field of vision and look at yourself as if through a wide-angle lens.

Where do you stand within a bigger group? Where do you stand within the people of your age? Where do you stand within the people who graduated from the same school as you, or everyone who works in the same field as you?

In this way I want you to adopt a slightly wider perspective. Then please think carefully about whether your situation is really as unfortunate as being hit by a meteorite.

Ascertain whether your perspective is true from the viewpoint of probability

You may be troubled that you cannot get promoted to section manager although you are already forty. But you need to know that in a company, not everyone can become a section manager. Usually, if you look at the scale of a business, you can roughly tell how many people will be able to become section managers.

In a manufacturing company, not even one person in ten can become a section manager, or perhaps not even one person in twenty. There are also companies that require only a few management staff, and instead have a need for many specialized engineers, clerical staff and blue-collar workers, but not the "heads." If you work for such a company, upon joining it you undoubtedly knew that only one in ten or one in twenty people would probably get as far as section manager. This number must have already been obvious about twenty years ago. Since you, yourself, chose to join that company, you have to be aware to some extent that even though you are not a section manager, it does not mean that you are particularly incompetent.

Of course, in service industries comparatively more people get promotions, and in trading companies or banks, there are so many section managers that you are always bumping into them. But even so, only about half of the employees can become section managers and the rest cannot. Thus, for each company, you can get a rough idea of how many people will get promoted from an overall picture of that company.

As for the probability of becoming an executive or a board member, it is even less likely. In some companies, only one of those people who joined the company in the same year can become an executive or board member, or in other companies, maybe three. There are even companies that produce only one executive or one board member every three to five years or so.

If you look at the situation of your company statistically, you can see the probability of your becoming an executive, so it might be a good idea to do your calculations. You might say that unless you become the company president, you will be a failure.

But if your company has more than 5,000 employees, there is practically no chance of that. If the scale of your company is that big, you cannot become a company president through ability alone.

You may undoubtedly be very capable. But if, for example, your boss clings to his position for ten years or so, there is very little chance of you succeeding him. You may be able to move up if he retires at the right time, but as long as he clings to his position, you will have no chance. This is because, however elite you may be, you have no authority over the people who are above you. Even though you can manage the affairs of the personnel below you, you cannot manage your superiors.

Thus, it is possible that you may not be able to become company president for the sole reason that there is a capable person about two years ahead of you. This is not a question of ability. If a talented person is about ten years ahead of you, you might have a chance to move up because of the age gap, but having a talented superior one or two years ahead of you will cut your chances of becoming the president.

This can happen even if, in the past, a person who is less able than you has become president. Because there is an order of precedence, it is practically impossible to become a president if you are working in a company with thousands of employees. Objectively speaking, it is sometimes a matter of luck.

However, even if you did become a president, you might not always be happy. Your company could go bankrupt, putting you through tremendous difficulties.

In any case, you can get a fair idea of the probability of you becoming an executive, so you need to recognize the level of promotion that would be reasonable for you. If you think of your promotion as your own problem, it will no doubt become a serious issue for you. You need to look at your chances of promotion objectively, from the perspective of other people or from the overall picture. Then you will often find that your current position is appropriate after all.

Promotion sometimes leads to a slump

Moreover, there are people who were brilliant as subordinates but who, as managers, lack discernment. In other words, there are many people who are brilliant at following orders as subordinates, but when they become a section manager or general manager, they cannot handle the job. This is because different rules come into play and different abilities are required in their work.

For example, some people move up the ladder at top speed as far as section manager and become the first out of their group of recruits to get that far, but after that they cannot do so well. This type of person is extremely useful from his boss' point of view, and as soon as he is assigned a job he will respond with a "Yes!" and quickly complete his task. On the other hand, when it comes to making decisions about whether to proceed with a matter or not, he has no idea of how to work on it. In fact, the abilities required are of a different type.

Even though he was promoted so quickly to section manager, soon after reaching that position, he finds himself unable to do his work. For him, this may seem to be one of life's riddles. He may even feel like jumping off a bridge. Despite the fact that he was the first out of two hundred people in his recruit group to reach the position of section manager, and thought that he was on the fast track to becoming president, upon becoming section manager, he suddenly finds himself incompetent. What is more, he may gain a bad reputation and become unable to trust himself.

The abilities required change according to the position

In short, higher positions require different abilities. Up until then, the type of ability required had been simply to do the task he was personally responsible for, not that of making use of others to improve results.

Someone who excels at handling tasks sometimes finds, when he gets promoted, that he is incapable of making use of subordinates. Since he quickly thinks of how he would have done the work himself, he orders his subordinates to do it in the same way. However, others are not like him and cannot do that. So, for the first time he runs into the problem of how to get the work done using people who have only half or a third of his ability, to which he has never given any thought before.

Of course, since he was more competent than others, he was promoted more quickly. But naturally, as he moves up the corporate ladder, he will then have to use people with only half or a third of his ability. He may be tempted to solve that problem by firing them, but it is not as easy as that, because he cannot form a team of subordinates whose abilities are on par with his. If all his subordinates were as competent as him, he would not have been promoted in the first place. He was promoted because he is more talented than the others, so he must use people who are not as able as he is.

Whether the subordinates have half or a third of his talent, if he leaves them idle, their contribution will be zero. If he not only leaves them idle but also lets them obstruct the flow of work, their contribution is negative. So, even if they only have half or a third of his ability, he has to put his subordinates to work, otherwise the company will not get any return on paying their salaries.

At such times, if he cannot change his way of thinking and just gets irritated about why they cannot handle work the way that he can, he will remain unable to use those staff. Naturally, the subordinates will feel that their boss does not rate them highly and, as a result, the relations between them will worsen.

Eventually he will have had enough and take all of his subordinates off the job and, as section manager, take over all of the work himself saying, "Look how hard I work! I must be appreciated!" He will then try to do the work of ten people. But, as he has only one body, even if he works nonstop all day long, there is no way he can handle the clerical work of ten or twenty people. Finally, he will damage his health and end up collapsing or being hospitalized. These are "the tragedies of middle management," which occur in the age group of section managers and general managers.

In fact, he is required to develop different abilities. In the world of sports, it is often said that a great player will not necessarily be a good coach. If he has to use people more mediocre than himself, or people with obvious faults, being at their best is crucial.

Essentially, before becoming a manager, you need to understand a manager's job and observe how the people above you are making use of other employees. In this way, learn how to be a leader. You must keep on learning this for two or three years. If you are promoted without this preparation, tragedy tends to strike.

I feel sorry for people who face such tragedies, but that too demonstrates the limits of their ability. They hit their limit when different abilities are required of them. Different abilities are required on each rung of the corporate ladder, including general manager, director general, executive and other positions. So you need to know that when you are promoted, you cannot always win approval for the abilities that were highly evaluated before your promotion.

Abilities that can only be demonstrated once you are promoted to a managerial position

There is also the opposite case where a very capable person cannot demonstrate his abilities in his first three to five years of work with the company when he is only doing office work. While his superiors know that this kind of thing can often happen, he himself is frustrated at being unable to do office work very well.

For example, nowadays many university graduates can neither use an abacus, nor do bookkeeping unless they have studied in a department of commerce. So if they join a traditional company of long standing and are suddenly handed an abacus and told to do calculations, of course, they cannot do them. Having hardly ever used a calculator, many of them suffer for years because they must do something that they have never studied.

When it comes to office work, you may find many people can do better than you. But when it comes to people who have studied advanced subjects, it usually takes years before their abilities are recognized. If you are of this type, you need to understand this beforehand. When you reach an age where you are in charge of other people, you need to use abilities that require discernment to make decisions. But such abilities are not really needed nor appreciated while you are still being entrusted with miscellaneous tasks. So you need fortitude, or the strength to persevere.

Don't be shortsighted - open your eyes to the overall picture

In the previous sections, I made the following two points: firstly, be aware that many of the people who experience slumps are of excellent character. Secondly, if you fall into a slump and become extremely troubled or anguished, think about how competent you are in relation to the whole of society.

This applies not only to companies but also to schools. For some reason, bright students want to go to schools where bright people gather, so they choose one that hundreds of bright students attend and dare to experience a sense of inferiority. I wonder why they choose to go there, since they will only develop an inferiority complex. Although they could go to other schools, upon seeing the people who are brighter than them gathering, they too want to go there. As a result, they will be teased or completely defeated.

Cram schools nowadays classify students in minute detail according to their scores and suggest they go to the schools most appropriate to their scores. Students tend to aim too high and take the entrance examination of higher-level schools, hoping by chance to pass. But even if they succeed in passing the exam, in many cases they cannot keep up with their studies and have a very hard time after entering those schools.

In worldly terms, this may be the same as wanting to join a major corporation. Just as people are admired because they work for a famous company, if they go to a prestigious school they will be praised. That is why they want to enter such schools, but whether or not they will be happy at those schools is a different matter.

There are many people who have been competing ever since they were in kindergarten or elementary school, and sometimes they are still doing so even as they work for a company. Such people seem to be riding an express train to unhappiness.

It is very common for people who have been crushed by excessive competition to suffer from mental or physical illness such as psychosomatic disorders, and they are often completely exhausted. For this reason, even if they are graduates of a top-class university, after they have joined a company, they hit a brick wall; they cannot come up with any good ideas to improve their work, are always in bad shape and have no dreams. In reality, there are many people like this but people still keep on competing with others, believing that they will only win if they can get onto an elite track. I feel rather sorry for such people.

They tend to be like this probably because they can only see things shortsightedly, so please expand your field of vision a little. It would be better to assume a slightly more defiant attitude.

It is also important not to push yourself too hard. Recently cram schools have become aware of this, and give students advice like, "Don't push yourself too hard. It is better to choose a school one rank lower. You'll find your studies easier there." They have seen a lot of cases in the past where, although students stretched themselves to enter their first choice of school, afterwards they couldn't catch up with their studies. It is certainly true that there are good aspects to a competitive society, but many people are crushed too soon by it. So you need to consider these aspects carefully as well.

The same holds true for companies. If you choose a fiercely competitive company, you are hardly likely to get promoted, whereas if you join a slightly lower-ranked company, there is a higher possibility of promotion. But of course, if you aim too low you will most likely be dissatisfied working there.

In any event, it is better to look at things in the context of the big picture. It is not good to consider things within the confines of a narrow world. For example, as we grow up, we become aware that everyone's ranking of standardized tests does not necessarily indicate the ranking of abilities. If the tests were held weekly, results would turn out in a completely different order. So it is nonsense to believe that rankings from school days apply throughout an entire lifetime. You need to be careful of this point.

4. A Chance to Discover a New Self

Cultures that cannot adapt to the changing times will perish

Nowadays people are pointing out that Japanese society is eroding, but the fact is that the old system is now collapsing. In the post-war period of high growth, once people had joined an organization, their position was guaranteed until retirement. Just like how buying a ticket at the first station enables you to ride the train to the last stop. There used to be such a fixed system. However, that culture is now breaking down.

There are probably far too many people who still adhere to the traditional Japanese culture with characteristics such as lifetime employment and the seniority system. They cannot cope with these changing times. However, unless we crush this culture, we will soon be unable to keep up with these times of change.

In the old Japanese navy, there was a system called the "hammock number," where everyone's number was determined by their ranking, according to their grades at the time of their graduation from the naval academy. This number was inscribed on their hammock. So, the hierarchy was decided at the time of graduation, and promotions were given in order of precedence.

In wartime, however, whether you win in battle is based on capability, not on grades. The person with the best grades would not always beat the person with second-best grades. Rather, in actual combat, the result is often the opposite. In battle, it is often the case that people who are not so intellectual can win by animal instinct, while intellectuals lose because they think too much.

In the Japanese military and naval academy, cadets were obliged to study and memorize the details of past wars, and were then tested on them. Therefore, those who had memorized the events of past wars could answer properly and get high scores. If a question was about past wars and how these wars could have been won, they could write an answer explaining in detail. In reality, however, no one, including the teachers, is able to write a model answer about wars that will occur in the future. That is to say, there was no way of gauging a cadet's ability to deal with a battle that would take place in the future.

Although it is a very difficult challenge, in today's society we are required to have this ability to cope with future events.

German officers insisted that Ieyasu Tokugawa should have lost

From Japanese history, take a look at the Battle of Sekigahara* that occurred in 1600. It was a major battle between Ieyasu Tokugawa's** eastern army and Mitsunari Ishida's*** western army. Each took up their positions on the battlefield, with practically the same number of troops, though there were slightly more in the western army.

Later, in the Meiji Era (the late 19th century to early 20th century), some German officers were invited to Japan from the German Military Headquarters to provide the Japanese with military training. When they were shown the battle formations, they all said that the western army would win.

The Japanese explained, "No, that's not what happened. So-and-so betrayed them and the western army lost." But apparently the German officers insisted,

* The Battle of Sekigahara: Most decisive battle during the Sengoku period, in the year 1600, in Sekigahara (Gifu Prefecture). Many Daimyō split and fought on either the western or the eastern Army. The eastern Army led by Ieyasu Tokugawa achieved victory, giving rise to Tokugawa Shogunate.

** Ieyasu Tokugawa (1543 - 1616): Founder and the first Shogun of Tokugawa Shogunate (Edo Bakufu). Ieyasu was appointed as Shōgun in 1603 and marked the start of Edo period which remained in power for over 260 years until the Meiji Restoration.

*** Mitsunari Ishida (1560 - 1600): Military commander during the Sengoku period. He led the western Army during the Battle of Sekigahara, and was defeated by Tokugawa's eastern Army.

"No, even if there was treachery, this battle was winnable from the west. With this battle formation, it is unbelievable that the western army did not win. Tactically speaking, the western army had to have won. We don't understand why it lost."

While the Battle of Sekigahara took place more than 400 years ago, modern military strategists from Germany in its prime around 100 years ago looked at the battle formations and said that the western army would win. So you can never know the outcome unless a battle is actually fought.

From a religious perspective, the reason the eastern army won was Ieyasu's spiritual power. Put simply, there was a disparity between the spiritual powers of the top leaders. There was probably not enough spiritual power or luck on Mitsunari's side or, to put it another way, he did not have the ability to captivate people's souls and draw the chance of victory to his side. On the contrary, Ieyasu did have the spiritual power and the willpower to achieve it.

In any case, people who have the power to win will win, and that is a strength forged on the battlefield. In that sense, however scientifically you can analyze a battle and predict which army will win or lose within the conditions of a certain terrain, formations and numbers of troops, the result can be different when the battle is actually fought.

What counts the most in actual combat is an instinct for victory. After all, Ieyasu once defeated Hideyoshi* at the Battle of Komaki and Nagakute, when Hideyoshi was at the height of his powers. It was a minor battle, but defeating Hideyoshi became the source of Ieyasu's confidence and charisma. In fact, after that he was known as "the man who defeated Hideyoshi."

At that time, it produced a general assumption that because even Hideyoshi could not beat him, there was no way that Hideyoshi's subordinates could amass troops and win. Thus, everyone naturally thought that since the general himself lost to Ieyasu, anyone of lower rank would not be able to win. This being the case, even if all the military experts insisted that the western army would win, it would most likely lose. In actual combat, such forces come into play.

The U.S. Navy triumphed because of promotion based on a merit system. Even if people were promoted to commander-in-chief on account of their ranking in a class at the naval academy at the time of their graduation, they could not necessarily win in battle. In contrast to the Japanese system, in the United States, those who were competent were promoted according to a stringent meritocracy. For example, there was a cadet who got average grades in the naval academy and

* Hideyoshi Toyotomi (ca, 1537 - 1600): Military commander during the Sengoku period. Born as a son of a peasant, he gained power, unified Japan, and was promoted to Kampaku, the chief advisor to the emperor. He is famous for his gain in power.

became an admiral in the end. From this, we can see that the U.S. Navy promoted people who were strong in actual combat. In this respect, the U.S. Navy is superior.

After the war, Japan changed slightly, perhaps influenced by the U.S. But still, the wartime culture that was based on steady, seniority-based promotion persisted in Japan, and that culture is now being broken down.

How to cope when the old ways no longer work

It is important to possess the strength to adapt yourself to such changes. If you are in a slump at the moment, you need to be aware of what type of person you are. Although you may have thought that you were competent, maybe you were just a good runner only when there was a pre-determined course where everybody knew the route. Maybe you were not able to exert your full powers on unmarked tracks.

Traveling the untrodden path requires producing new additional value, which is something that academic types find hard to do. Highly intelligent people like to analyze previous patterns, then ponder and memorize them. But they are not good at producing answers about future events on their own. This is because their thinking tends to be too inflexible, and they are too attached to previous patterns.

So, you need to have the power to break through the old patterns. Sometimes the old patterns need to be kept, but when necessary you must break through them. Even if you have been told to follow the old patterns by your boss, you must skillfully destroy them, otherwise your company will not grow. In troubled times, this kind of ability is required.

If you have fallen into a slump because you have reached a deadlock with your abilities or old methods of working, then you need to change your way of thinking. You may think that it is best to keep your old methods that led to success. But if these methods no longer work and you find yourself in a slump, maybe the time has come to change your ways. Perhaps you are now being given the time to discover new ways.

After all, you are the only one who can break through the wall that is blocking you. You must have the courage to break out of your shell and transform yourself.

In terms of Happy Science, for example, we can act as intellectuals but at the same time we also have a wild side, which prompts us to take "barbaric" actions. That is Happy Science's strength. Nobody knows which side will predominate, so to people outside the organization, we are quite unpredictable.

However, this is something that we are doing intentionally, because otherwise we will soon hit a brick wall. If we always follow the same pattern, everyone gets comfortable and tends to have similar sorts of thought patterns all the time. Then, when circumstances change, we will be unable to break down the obstacles that arise. That is why we sometimes crush the old patterns. We dare to do things that most people would object to, like revealing our "barbaric" side or acting recklessly, and in this way we try to change our mindsets.

So, if you are feeling depressed and at a dead-end, I believe it is also important to recognize that a chance to transform yourself is being given.

After experiencing the chrysalis period you can become a butterfly

The first thing I told you to bear in mind when you are in a slump is to become aware of the fact that you are of great character.

The second was to think about how you rank overall. I want you to look at your position statistically. For example, if you are a student, consider how you would rank amongst tens of thousands of students, not just within the range of a specific group or just within your school. If you are working in a company, think about the average position of the thousands or tens of thousands of staff in total. I talked of the importance of taking this kind of total picture into consideration.

The third point I made was that sometimes success cannot be attained while holding on to old methods.

Some people do not realize this and struggle in a slump, thinking that they have hit a dead-end or are in a rut. So I told you to think of a slump as a chance to discover a new "you;" a chance for you to transform and innovate yourself. In other words, although you may think that you are in bad condition, that may not be the case. Perhaps it is just that you need to change your ways or you need to discover a new self.

At such times, you may think, "I have given my best, but to no avail. This must be the limit of my abilities," but in fact there is another way of looking at it: maybe it's time to make a change. If you transform yourself, a new path will open up.

For example, while a caterpillar crawls along a branch or along the ground, it may be proud of itself. As it speeds along a branch and munches on leaves, the caterpillar may be content, believing, "I'm an elite caterpillar." However, one day its body stiffens and it can no longer move. The caterpillar is completely bewildered by this, thinking, "What's happening? I've turned into a chrysalis. Is my life going to end like this?" But, in fact, a time will come when its hard skin splits open and the chrysalis turns into a butterfly and takes off into the sky.

Perhaps a slump is equivalent to the time in a chrysalis. It must be truly painful for an elite caterpillar to experience a time when it can no longer move. As its body stiffens and weakens, it probably feels, "What's going on?

What's going to happen to me? Am I going to mummify and die like this?" However, before long it sprouts wings and a completely unexpected new self will emerge.

Then the butterfly will find that it can fly. It may think, "Hey, I can fly. I thought that being elite means to be able to crawl quickly along a branch, but now I can soar in the blue skies. That's really cool. I still have a future after all." It would not know until it actually happens. As a caterpillar, it would not understand that. So, even if it experiences the time in a chrysalis, eventually it will transform itself and fly off into the skies. I'm sure that is truly a great feeling.

To humans, butterflies may seem less happy because they are not highly intelligent and cannot think about advanced matters. But the delight they experience flying, may be greater than that of humans. Humans cannot fly unless they sit in an aircraft and, to a butterfly, machines like helicopters may seem ridiculously clumsy and unsightly. Butterflies may be thinking, "How embarrassing, flailing around like that!" and pitying humans for being unable to fly freely through the air on their own and having to rely on such awkward machines.

Certainly, butterflies can soar through the air without any fuel, and they can fly all the way from Taiwan to Japan riding the winds. This is an easy task for them; unlike an aircraft, they have no need for fuel. I imagine that butterflies feel great happiness flying freely across the sky

A slump is also an opportunity to transform into a new person

Humans also experience the stages of "caterpillar," "chrysalis" and "butterfly." So, even if you fear that your life is over, perhaps that is just the "chrysalis" stage for you. You may be in the "chrysalis" stage, or in other words, a period of preparation to create a new self.

In the same way that a chrysalis cannot move, during a slump, you will find that everything is in shambles, no new ideas arise and you are unable to feel like taking action. You may sometimes be near depression and try to shut yourself away from the world. However, this might just be a temporary chrysalis phase. Once you get through it, you may then turn into a butterfly.

You have probably never thought of yourself turning into a butterfly, but please try to imagine it. I would like you to think that this may be a chance to become a new "you." After all, everyone must pass through the chrysalis stage in order to achieve further growth and success. You cannot go on living unless your old self dies.

People nowadays can live eighty or ninety years, so they will undergo this sort of experience several times in their lives. They will find that their past self-image crumbles, they plunge into a state of confusion and have little ability to see the future, but then they are finally born anew. They cannot stay the same throughout their lives. They must experience this period of transformation at least two or three times during their lives, otherwise they will not succeed in the current age.

You may think that you have been doing well and there is no need to change, but that is the same as the caterpillar being proud of its ability to crawl. I want you to consider the possibility of growing wings and flying. If you think that you are in the chrysalis stage, you will be able to save your strength and bide your time. During that time, rather than simply doing nothing, it is essential to build up your strength and make preparations, little by little, as inspiration guides you.

It often happens that what you think is a slump is in fact a time to make the shift to a new self. I, myself, have experienced this many times. In some ways, it cannot be helped. No matter how much you struggle, nothing can be done until the times change and a new situation emerges. During that time, you will be impatient searching for a way out and it is indeed painful, but all you can do is bide your time.

Once time passes, things will certainly change. Many things will change including human relationships, and a completely new stage will suddenly emerge. It truly is a mystery, but that's the way it is. So, when you are in a slump, think that you are in the chrysalis stage and wait for the coming opportunity to transform yourself. This is also a very important way of overcoming a slump. Please be a person who can think in this way.

5. How to Cope with a Slump

(Method 1) Focus on your current worries

During a slump, in many cases, all you can do is endure. But when I look back at my own experiences and think about how I dealt with slumps, I found that there are several other approaches.

- Nothing can be done about hang-ups from the past or worries about the future

First of all, during a slump you are often obsessed with hang-ups from the past, and think endlessly about worries or matters that cannot be changed. During that time, you are also concerned about the future, and anguish over events in the future that have yet to happen. While you are stuck in the current situation, you spend much time fretting over hang-ups from the past or worrying about the future. In most cases, people in slumps are in terrible anguish, fixating on the past and the future.

In short, you are anguishing over matters about which you can do nothing. In most cases you are worrying about a past that cannot be changed and a future that nothing can be done about. But, in reality, you are living in the "present," a moment between the past and the future. So, as I said in the previous section about the chrysalis stage, you sometimes need to look at your life in segments of time; in a flow of past, present and future. This is one approach to overcome slumps.

- The technique of the swordsman Musashi Miyamoto: defeating opponents one by one

When you are in a slump, you are not in the best condition, so it is a time to be on the defense. During slumps, you cannot win if you fight several different worries at the same time. If you take on many "opponents" simultaneously when you are in poor shape, you will not be able to win.

Take, for example, a famous Japanese swordsman Musashi Miyamoto.* He fought many people, but he always tried to fight only one opponent at a time. He fought more than sixty times during his life, and won all of them.

One reason he could win was that he was fleet of foot. If he fought against several opponents at the same time, at some point he would be struck and cut down, so he would run. Naturally, his enemies would chase

* Musashi Miyamoto (1578 - 1645): Swordsman and samurai, famous for his duels and fighting style. He is also the author of *The Book of Five Rings*, a book on strategy, tactics and philosophy.

after him, but as their speeds were too different, the enemies would spread out. Then, he would deal with each one individually, starting with the fastest one. Thus, by running he got his enemies to spread out and always fought a single opponent.

Musashi also prevented himself from being surrounded and fought, for example, with his back against the wall. He sometimes made surprise attacks, too. He was a fast runner, had plenty of stamina and very strong arms, so he put up a good fight, using the tactic of defeating one enemy at a time. If attacked from all sides by four different enemies, he would certainly have lost, even if he had been able to fight with a sword in each hand. That's why he always got his opponents to scatter, so that he could not be surrounded and made helpless. He would thus secure a good position from which to fight while taking on his opponents individually.

When he was chased, for example, he would run uphill and then when his opponents got out of breath, he would cut them down. Therefore, as long as he was able to keep his breath, he would surely win. In this way, he put his opponents at a disadvantage and defeated them one by one.

Needless to say, as a religion, we are not encouraging people to kill others. When I say, "Always fight your enemies one at a time," I'm making the analogy as one way of thinking, so please do not misunderstand and think that I'm telling you to kill people.

The point is that it is no use battling against the problems from the past or the future at this moment. There may be several of these problems, maybe five or ten problems from the past, and five or ten problems about the future, which are now influencing you and causing you to suffer.

(Method 2) List your current worries and put them in order

Even if you fight with a "sword" in both hands, you can never win against all of these "enemies." First of all, you must scatter your "enemies" and defeat them one at a time. You cannot win unless you reduce the fight as much as possible, and against one opponent.

Thus, for the moment, let us take a huge pair of scissors and cut off the past and the future. There is no point in thinking about them now. There is nothing you can do about past mistakes and failures, so just put them aside for the moment. As for the future, it stretches on and on, into next year and the year after next, and once you start thinking about it, you will have far too many worries to deal with, so let's put them aside for the moment as well.

For the moment, just create an enclosure around "present time" and only look at the problems you are currently dealing with. Furthermore, since there are probably a number of problems that you need to face, count to see how many worries you actually have. Of course, there would be not just one, but maybe five or ten. Then, prioritize these problems and resolve them in turn, one at a time. It is also important to sort them into big problems and small problems, in other words, to separate the important issues from the trivial ones.

You could also use the principle of fragmenting. This can be explained using the analogy of clearing snow off a roof. The roof cannot be cleared all at once, but you can scoop up small portions of snow with a shovel and gradually clear it all off.

With these methods, you can break your current "enemies" into pieces and get rid of them one at a time. How many of these worries do you have right now? You have to count them, think of a way to disperse them and defeat them one by one, just like Musashi Miyamoto did.

(Method 3) Sort out each problem in turn

- Solving the fundamental problem first

When you set out to solve your worries, you may think about how and where to start. One method is to defeat your most powerful enemy first.

In battle, for example, if you cut down the enemy's general first, the rest will lose their fighting spirit and become disheartened. Even if there are sixty enemies, once their general has been defeated, the entire group will fall into confusion. When that happens, you can make your escape while felling the enemies who have scattered one by one. This is one way of thinking. In terms of the law of priority, this is equivalent to the method of solving the most basic problem first.

- Solving the problem that seems simplest first

Another method is to see which of your problems would be the easiest to solve and sort that one out first. From the viewpoint of the spirit world, this is a method that demons often use. In fact, demons aim for the weak points when they attack. Regardless of whether this method is righteous or not, it can also be applied as a rule of life, so you can use it when solving problems.

For example, sometimes you can be entangled in five problems you have and your mind is completely caught up in them. At such times, discern which of the five problems is the easiest to solve, select the "puny one" and solve that one first. This will reduce your problems to four. You then select the next easiest issue and solve that. With this, you now have three problems remaining.

As you reduce the number of problems in this way, the most momentous problem will seem to lighten a little, as if a fog has cleared away. Certainly, that problem itself is still a serious one, but sometimes it seems even more difficult and complicated when other problems are tangled up with it, so you should first remove all entanglements.

I would not call this approach "the law of demons," but rather it may be similar to the law that governs the world of carnivores. For example, when lions or tigers attack prey such as antelope, they go for those that are slow and cannot escape in time, such as the very young, the sick, or the injured. If this rule were adopted in combat, it would be the method of defeating the seemingly weak enemies first. In problem solving, it would be equivalent to reducing the number of worries by eliminating the easiest ones first.

- Use the "principle of fragmentation" for big problems

In the end, you will be left with the problem that seems the biggest. If it were a company management problem, it would be very serious and extremely complicated. When it comes to overall management problems, you should use the "principle of fragmentation" and break the problem up into smaller parts.

Just agonizing over what you should do, as if you were mulling over a Zen koan, will not do any good. So in such cases, you have to break the problem down and ascertain where the root of it lies. Is it a human resources problem? Is it a debt problem? Or is the trouble caused by a lack of ability to develop new products? Is it a problem of not being able to collect payments despite the fact that you have made sales? Perhaps you are weak when it comes to collecting payments. Or, is it because a rival has emerged and you are losing customers?

It is possible to break down even a management problem in this way. Although you may have thought it was a huge problem, when you break it down you will find that it fragments into several smaller ones. Then, if you have the ability to do this, you can choose the most important issue and deal with it or, if you cannot, sort them out one at a time, starting with the one that seems the easiest to solve.

Getting through times when, for some reason, you are not at your best

I will do a quick recap of what I have just taught you.

First of all, separate your current worries from worries about the past or the future. Eliminate the latter and focus only on problems that are happening now.

Then, out of the problems that you are involved in, list the ones that are solvable depending on how you approach them. There may be five or ten of these.

Attack the biggest problem if you think you currently have the ability to solve it, and annihilate it. Once that is done, you can get rid of the scattered, remaining problems.

If you lack the ability to solve the biggest worry, there is also the method of reducing the number of problems by solving the easiest one first. Then, when the biggest problem is left, break it down into yet smaller problems, and you can either sort out the major problem first or the peripheral ones.

Of course, if you have the power to bulldoze your way through these, that is great but if not, all you can do is open up a path with a shovel in hand. When you have no chance of winning, that is the only way to fight. Adopt the tactic of focusing your attack on a few enemies for the time being, and reduce the actual number of enemies.

If you categorize your problems like this and try to solve them, to some extent you will be able to get out of a slump, a time when somehow you are not at your best.

Example: Overcoming a baseball slump

- Analyze why you cannot hit the ball and think about where to attack

As I mentioned earlier, there are times when the cleanup batter or a .300 hitter cannot hit the ball. What must be done at such times is to analyze the reasons why you are missing the ball, think from many different angles about what you can do to improve your scores. Then start tackling the aspects that you think you can improve.

For example, do you have any trouble with your batting form? Do you usually have a healthy diet? Do you have any worries, such as sickness of a family member? Or could the reason be that a new rival has appeared and is doing better than you? Is it because the opponents' pitchers have found your weak points?

Certainly, if one opponent spots your weaknesses and discovers that you cannot hit high and inside balls, other pitchers will start following suit. As a result, you may no longer be able to hit the ball because everyone pitches aiming for your weak point.

There must be various reasons for your troubles, so you need to analyze them carefully and see which part of the problem you can tackle. When a home run batter is in a slump, it's better for him not to aim for a home run but just focus on trying to hit the ball. As he continues making it out to first base, after a while he may be able to recover his form.

Apart from these, there are various other methods such as shutting yourself away in a Zen temple or practicing swinging a Japanese sword. Some people actually use these methods. You should also find your own ways of solving your problem.

Please note that you must first cut away the worries about the past and the future, and limit yourself to your current worries. Then focus on a specific issue to deal with. Unless you adopt this approach, it is not very easy to find a solution.

- Know your ability based on your past "batting average" and have confidence

As we are using a baseball batter as our example, we should also take the "batting average" into consideration. In other words, you need to see your abilities objectively and know how well you can do based on your past performances.

Take, for example, Sadaharu Oh,* who was a very famous home run batter in Japan. When he was still an

* Sadaharu Oh (1940 -): Retired Japanese professional baseball player and manager. The holder of a home run record of 868. In 2006, Oh led Japan's national baseball team to win the WBC championship.

active baseball player, he often went a month without hitting a home run. Strangely enough, it is usually people like him who experience a lot of slumps. He could not perform well consistently. Although he could hit many home runs when he was on form, there were also times when he would go for a month with no home runs. It was quite pitiful to watch him in a slump, but if we looked at the season overall he always set a reasonable record.

In fact, in more than a hundred games in a season, capable batters can hit 30 or 40 home runs in total. But they don't know when. They may hit these home runs in the spring, summer or autumn. Nevertheless, even if they have times when they cannot hit a ball, if we look at the entire year, a .300 batter will hit 30% of the balls, and someone who has the ability to hit 40 home runs will do so on average throughout the year, even if they cannot hit the ball over certain periods of time, say, in the month of June or August. But over the year as a whole, they will find that they have reasonable results, based on the law of batting averages.

When you are in a slump, you tend to be contemptuous of yourself and think that you are no good. However, you need to make an objective assessment of your own ability and think, "Although I'm in a slump at the moment, I know I can do this much and I am worthy of this kind of evaluation." It is important to have this objective yardstick.

Even if your current rating or performance is too low measured against that yardstick, at some point you will recover your form and compensate for it by improving your record. That time will surely come. So accordingly, you need to have self-confidence.

Of course, most people are not baseball batters, but a similar thing can also happen in the field of inventions, for instance. Even if there are times when you cannot invent anything at all, after a while ideas will start to well up. Therefore, you need to look at your "batting average" in your own field and have confidence in your abilities based on your work so far and the knowledge of what you should be capable of.

Although your work may be awful now and you may not get satisfactory results, your performance will improve at some time. If it does not resolve within a year, average out over a span of three years or so and you will find that you are being evaluated at a level that corresponds to your real abilities. Even if you cannot do well for six months or so, you will suddenly be able to do much better after a while and, if you average your work out over a year or maybe three, you will find that you have done almost the same level of work. If your performance was better than your average, it means that your average itself has risen.

Therefore, it is important not to get desperate when you are not in form. Rather, be aware of your average level of competence and have trust in it. You cannot always perform at your best, so you always need to be aware of your own average.

6. Overcoming the Worst-Case Scenario

First of all, be prepared to accept the worst

When I was young, I learned a great deal from the books of Dale Carnegie. He wrote in one of his books that it is important to be prepared to accept the worst. This, too, is a form of wisdom.

In his book, there is a passage that says something along the lines of, "When it comes to the worries you currently have, first ask yourself: What is the worst that can happen? Then prepare to accept it. Once you adopt that attitude, your mind will not waver so much. After that, calmly consider whether there are any ways to improve the worst-case scenario even slightly." This, too, is a good approach and I found it extremely helpful.

So first of all, you should consider the worst-case scenario that you could be faced with at the present point in time. From all past, present and future angles, think about what is the worst possible situation that could arise concerning the problem you are facing now. Then accept this and make up your mind, thinking, "Even if the worst comes to the worst, I'll somehow manage to overcome it."

For example, what would happen if your company went bankrupt? That certainly would not mean that all the employees would suddenly die. There would still be a way forward by changing occupations.

Or let's imagine that you have made a huge mistake in your work and are scared that you might be fired. In such a situation, the worst-case scenario is that you will be forced to leave the company for corporate restructuring. However, if you could accept that conclusion, you will be able to think, "Other paths may open up for me. I don't have any specific company in mind yet. But, with my current skills there must be other places where I can work."

Another example is that a member of your family falls ill and dies. You may be upset if your father or mother gets cancer, but in modern-day society that happens to about one in three families. In a sense, such occurrences are perfectly natural and could happen anywhere. It might have been totally unexpected for you, but in any case all humans are subject to disease and cancer is a very common cause of death. So it can sometimes happen. Even so, it comes as a tremendous shock to you.

Sometimes, you or your spouse may get cancer. Sometimes it is curable and sometimes it is not. In such a case, ultimately all you can do is to accept it. It can happen that a member of your family dies, or you, yourself, might die. There is no one reading this book, for example, who will be alive 100 years from now. Almost everyone will be dead. Everyone must eventually die and it is just a matter of whether it is sooner or later.

Given that, all you can do is accept the fact of cancer and the worst-case scenario, resolve to study the other world diligently and cultivate a peaceful mind. Things will be easier if you are prepared to die in this way. You may be worried about what will happen to your family and work after you die, but just let it go, thinking, "Everything is going to be all right." If you accept the worst-case scenario in this way and then think calmly, you will often be able to find some measures to take.

Examples of cancer patients living a long life

In countries such as the United States, terminal cancer patients are told of their illness. According to a survey, even if everyone equally is told of their illness, the number of years that they continue living differs from person to person.

For example, people who, upon learning of their illness, become frantic about the short time they have left and immerse themselves in hard work will die fairly early on. People who lament bitterly when they hear they have cancer and give in to despair also die quickly.

On the other hand, there are also people who, when told that they have cancer, think, "So its cancer is it? I suppose it was inevitable. In life, sometimes you have to know when to give up, so I guess I must accept it and get on with it. I'll just take it easy and savor the rest of my life." Unexpectedly, these kinds of people do not die so easily.

In other words, those who unexpectedly live longer than their doctor had predicted are the people who give in to their fate, who come to terms and live with it thinking, "Getting cancer is just part of my life. Apparently one in three people get it anyway so I'm going to lead the rest of my life calmly and peacefully." On the other hand, people who turn to working really hard and people who gravely lament their lot seem to die sooner.

Apparently there are these three patterns to people's reactions, but there are also a few exceptions. These are people who firmly believe that it is impossible for them to have cancer. They try hard to keep hypnotizing themselves, "It isn't cancer! I haven't got cancer! I'm fine! I'm healthy!" Sometimes such people also live longer than predicted.

This is similar to what is happening in the world of religion, and indeed it actually happens among members of Happy Science. I've heard that some of our members lead long lives while continuing to hypnotize themselves with such words. Sometimes other-dimensional power is at work and the illness cures completely, but this is rather exceptional. (Note: Cases of patients miraculously recovering from terminal cancer or incurable diseases are increasing year after year. This is in relation to the increase in the power of faith.)*

Generally speaking, it seems that people who try too hard and people who take the matter too grimly tend to die soon, while people who accept what happened and come to terms with their cancer tend to lead longer lives.

Religion makes it possible to overcome the fear of death

The worst-case scenario can sometimes occur but if you accept it, you can still find another path of life.

Perhaps you can think of various worst-case scenarios, such as losing all your possessions, your company or work, but the saddest thing that remains to the end is probably that you, yourself, will die. In Happy Science, however, we teach about the world after death and, since our basic teachings are built upon the

---

* See *Secrets of the Everlasting Truths*, IRH Press Co., Ltd., *A Method for Superb Health* (tentative title), IRH Press Co., Ltd., available only in Japanese, and other publications.

fact that death awaits us all, you do not need to be so scared of dying. If you can think, "That's why I joined Happy Science and I'm studying its teachings," then the problem of death has already been solved for you.

All you have to do now is to improve your state of mind in the remaining days so that you can go back to as high a heavenly realm as possible after you die. The amount of time you have left could be months or years, but within that time, you should improve your state of mind to go back to a better place. Set the direction of your effort and, while accepting death, try your best without pushing yourself too much. Lead your life in a way that does not trouble the people around you or torment you.

Put simply, if you have run out of ways to get out of a slump, you should finally accept the worst. This may be bankruptcy in the case of a company, dismissal in the case of a job, the death of you or a family member in the case of illness, or failing exams in the case of a student. If you can create a mindset of accepting the worst in this way, there is nothing to be scared of. Ultimately, accept the worst-case scenario and then try looking for ways to improve the situation, even slightly. This alone will lead you to find a good solution.

In this chapter I have taught various ways to get out of a slump. I hope that they will be helpful to you.

CHAPTER TWO

Triumphing Over Trials

~ How to Live Your Life with No Regrets ~

Lecture given on July 20, 2013
at Sacred Shrine of Great Enlightenment, Taigokan
Tokyo, Japan

1. "Triumphing Over Trials" is an Extremely Important Attitude

If you lose your way, always choose the difficult path

In this chapter, I will discuss the theme "triumph over trials." This is a common theme, and also a universal theme in religion. Outside of the world of religion, "triumphing over trials" is an extremely important attitude to have as you make your way through life's various difficulties or your life in society in general. So, in this chapter, I am going to condense my current thoughts on this topic as much as possible.

First of all, looking back at the time when I was younger, I feel that by nature I was the type of person who liked the idea of triumphing over trials or overcoming hardships. As I have mentioned in a book that describes my junior high school days,* I really liked the expression, "make every effort to enter through the narrow door." I, myself, liked to choose the more difficult path whenever I was split between several decisions.

This expression comes from a verse in the Bible that says, "Wide is the gate and broad is the road that leads to destruction, and many enter through it. But small is the gate and narrow the road that leads to life, and only

---

* See *An Encouragement of Intellectual Living in Youth* (tentative title), IRH Press Co., Ltd, available only in Japanese.

a few find it." (Matthew 7:13-14) It was engraved upon my heart that the road to life was very narrow and that it was very hard to enter through that narrow gate. Time and again, I was impressed by these words. The mere fact that these words resonated with me surely indicates that I was a type of person who thought in this way.

In the course of our lives, we encounter various trials such as sufferings and troubles, but my view on life was not on how to avoid them skillfully. Neither was I satisfied merely to think, "I have survived without any problems," "I have led a quiet life," or "I have lived an uneventful life without making any serious mistakes." I had already perceived in my own way that one of the major themes in my life was to improve my soul or strengthen my mentality.

Looking at my life from then on, when I did not know which path to follow, I always chose the difficult one.

At the end of my life, I do not want to regret having dreams that were too small

In following that difficult path, I, of course, often could not achieve my goals because of my lack of ability, experience or effort and because I had encountered various practical obstacles. However, I think of it in the following way.

77

There are probably many people who set themselves big challenges and feel regret when they cannot attain their goals or achieve success. But compared to feeling regret at failure or a lack of success, a graver issue would be to look back at your life and regret the fact that your dreams were too small. When I face the final curtain, I most certainly wish to avoid regretting, "Well, I had a long life, but the dreams I had were much too small." I feel very strongly about that.

In most cases, people who have achieved great success regret that their dreams were too small. Take, for example, people who set themselves the objective of saving one million dollars (100 million yen) in the course of their lives. Many of them may eventually achieve that goal through experiencing various occupations. But after they accomplish that goal, some of them immediately lose their purpose in life. This is because there is no additional value attached to the goal itself of saving one million dollars.

It would be different if they aspired to save one million dollars for a specific purpose, but if their goal is simply to save a million dollars, once they have achieved it they are left with nothing more to do. After all, the one million dollars can be won in a lottery or obtained by moving up the corporate ladder and saving your earnings. It could also come from profits from shares or through setting up a new business.

However, if you had only pursued the goal of saving a million dollars, the regret you would feel before you die would not be the mistakes you had made in life, but that your dream was too small. Oftentimes, a dream that you had thought at the time was almost impossibly big, turns out to be not so big after all. That is because as time passes, you accumulate a lot of experiences and achievements. Prior to that, it often seems that the dream is far too difficult to achieve.

Therefore, you must fight against this weakness of the mind, a daunted mind, the fear of failure and becoming arrogant over small successes. You should rather feel ashamed of living inside a trivial dream, believing that you have only known success, whereas in fact you have merely avoided challenges.

Destiny always has the next gate ready

I introduced the expression "make every effort to enter through the narrow door." To young people, and particularly those in their teens, passing the entrance exam to get into a good school is one of life's hurdles and it probably seems like a major goal. Passing the exams to enter a junior high school, high school or university probably seems like an incredibly big hurdle.

However, people who have cleared these hurdles can clearly see that they were nothing more than steps to open up a path to their future job. Having passed the exams does not guarantee you success and, conversely, having failed does not determine your failure in the future. In the course of a lifetime, one gate after another will stand before you. So, although passing exams may seem like a really big goal for teenagers who are studying for them, their perspective will change with time.

The same can be said of successful Japanese people in the Meiji and Taisho eras, and in the early Showa era. We can see this by reading their biographies. Although these people were living in an age when everyone vigorously pursued professional advancement, not all of them necessarily raced headlong into success from their teenage years. In fact, the number of people who did so was very low.

There was hardly anyone who did not experience failures at all, who continually achieved the greatest success. Generally speaking, people who believe that they have only known success have stopped growing at that point in their lives.

When you are facing a trial you may suffer acute pain, but it is important not to hold on to such negative thinking, meaning a paltry attitude of tormenting yourself, or to have low self-esteem. It is necessary to make diligent efforts to break through various hardships.

Even if you are unsuccessful, destiny always has the next gate ready for you. So, the energy and effort you put in at that time will not be completely in vain.

This point is worth repeating. Exams have a passing mark, and if you do not get a certain score you will fail the exam. However, it is totally wrong to base success or failure solely on whether or not you score higher than the passing mark and are given a certificate of qualification. People sometimes miss the passing mark by one or two points, but that does not mean that they are a complete failure.

Even though you may not be able to pursue a particular path, the actual effort you have made is in no way meaningless. If you reflect on why you were unsuccessful, the next step to success will be prepared for you.

People who have experienced many successes or a great success are aware of this. What seemed like trials, difficulties or setbacks - or what you gained by battling your sense of inferiority, just as a silkworm spews out thread - will eventually transform into something different. Most successful people know of this from experience.

I'm not joking when I say, "The seeds of suffering will surely become the seeds of your next happiness." This really is true. In many cases, the fact that you did not achieve your goal provides the fuel for your next efforts. There is something sad about a way of life wherein someone succeeds easily in achieving some goal, boasts about it and seeks nothing more, or a life of merely basking in past glories.

You can always take on new challenges, no matter how old you are

I am now getting somewhat older, so I sometimes feel like making excuses or saying things like, "I used to be able to do that," or "I could do that when I was young," but I think I need to put the brakes on this, even if I cannot completely stop saying it.

No matter how much you say, "I used to be able to do that," it is not going to do you any good. What you should be asking yourself is, "Can I do it now?" or "Am I going to be capable of doing it from now on?"

I have experienced many times that, regardless of age or experience, if you make new efforts and challenge yourself, a path will open up. You can always take on new challenges, no matter how old you are. It is important to keep on challenging the unknown and trying to overcome it, just as you did in your teens.

Of course, if it is a goal with an extremely slim likelihood of success, even if you make an effort, it will not be all that effective. Even if you are in your late fifties like me and you suddenly aspire to participate in the Olympics and try to win a gold medal, I'm not really sure whether a sport that would make that possible exists.

If there were Olympic events for people over fifty such as gateball, it might be possible to become a champion. But generally speaking, it is very hard to win a gold medal in the Olympics unless you are in your twenties or so. It would probably be very hard to do in your fifties.

However, if it is a goal that is somewhat attainable if you have the brains and experience, and if this goal captures your interest and enthusiasm sufficiently, you can actually become quite good at that if you make the effort. That is possible regardless of your age.

I do not want to speak too pessimistically about sports and disappoint those of you who are making efforts in that field, so I will only talk a little more about this. Quite some time after launching Happy Science, I gained quite a lot of weight. In some ways, it had a slightly negative impact on my work, so I took up tennis again. But because I did not play for about twenty years, I was really rusty.

For the first year or so after I started playing again, I was not very good, and whenever I played against a male secretary with some tennis skills, I always lost. He would generally let me win one game but I would lose around three out of four games. However, after about four years, I became the better player.

Also, at that time, I was being coached by a professional and with him, I could manage a 600-stroke rally and a 100-stroke rally of smashes. He even asked me if I was intending to turn pro.

When it comes to stamina, I don't have much confidence. Even so, when I was in junior high school, I was a fairly good player. However, there had been a long break and I was rusty, but when I gave it another try, I was able to improve my skills to a certain point. These things are possible.

2. My Learning Experiences at the Trading Company

Differences in ability within a limited timeframe can be reversed in the long run

People who are not Happy Science believers probably do not know this, but I am focusing a lot of effort on teaching English in our organization and providing various forms of guidance.

When I was young, my feelings about English were self-confidence mixed with a sense of inferiority or frustration. Many bright people from rural areas may have been outstanding students in elementary or junior high school. But when they are in high school or about to enter university, they start to encounter a steady stream of really able students from all over the country. There are so many brilliant students that it makes you wonder just where they have all sprung from.

This makes the outstanding students from rural areas feel that there is something strange going on. Although in the past they thought that they really stood out and felt that they were far ahead of others, now students from all over the country have gradually caught up with them. The other students are all very smart.

This is one reason for me to think that democracy has got it right. People's abilities are pretty much the same, and almost anyone is capable of getting good results if they make the effort. So, surprisingly enough, when it comes to academic results, other students catch up with the students that once stood out.

In terms of academic level, when I was in elementary and junior high school, there was a gap of a few school years between me and the other students, but from high school onwards, other people gradually caught up with me, and I really felt that the others were also doing very well. That was a surprise to me. So anyone can do well in their studies if they make the effort.

Because this happens, education today opens up a path to jobs, and the democratic system whereby each person has one vote is valid. In practical terms, if everyone has potential, there is not much of a great gap between the potential of any two people. So, perhaps the difference is just a question of the level of the actual results they produce. Although there seems to be a gap if you look at it within a limited timeframe, there is little difference in people's overall abilities and people can change over a longer period of time.

The obstacle I encountered after graduating from university: trading jargon

Even if a junior high school student is very smart, it is usually hard for him to be an exceptional English student in comparison to a third-year high school student. Also, I learned from experience while working at a trading company that English cannot be mastered without studying.

I did study English a little at university, but it was not like studying English for university entrance examinations. In liberal arts, the emphasis was more on reading literature, such as the works of Shakespeare. When I went on to my major courses, I read works in English on politics, international issues and diplomacy. I became capable of understanding the English related to my field of study to a certain extent. That is why I did not expect to have an inferiority complex about my English after going out into the business world.

I happened to join a trading company, and when I started working there, it was a real shock to discover how bad I was at English. Some of the English used in trading companies are very different from the English we learn at school or what I learned in my political science studies. I did not realize that. So, there are English words used specifically in trading, but we do not learn these in high school. People who specialize in related academic subjects at university probably study them, but as my field of study was different, I had no idea that a kind of "traders' English" existed.

I was shocked at how many English words were not in the dictionary

At that time, Kenkyusha's New College English-Japanese Dictionary was the most popular in Japan and it was a widely used, authoritative English-Japanese dictionary. The edition during that time had around 56,000 headwords. But when I read documents in English at work and came across a word I did not understand, in most cases I could not find it in the dictionary. So frankly, when I first started out, I thought, "How can I be expected to know the meaning of words that aren't in the College Dictionary?"

However, I was truly amazed to find that the people around me seemed to have no problem at all understanding those English words. Even people who had graduated from little-known provincial universities, private universities or two-year colleges knew many of these English words if they were working there a little longer than me. I remember being a little shocked that everyone around me knew these words in English which I did not, or words that I could not find in the dictionary.

Thinking about it now, there is probably a set of specialized English words used in each field. In the field of science, for example, there must, of course, be many technical terms that are used; work involving chemical plants or construction plants will use a set of specific terms, too. If you work in trading, it is only natural that you encounter trading jargon, or jargon relating to foreign exchange, but it was a shock for me because I neither learned such words, nor could I find them in the dictionary.

As a result, everyone else seemed to be incredibly clever while I, on the other hand, although once confident about my English skills, suddenly felt as if I was no good at it.

You have to plug away at learning words you do not know

However, you should not let such things get you down too much. For the first six months or so at the company, I felt as if I was submerged in water. It was as if I had jumped into a pool and bumbled around for six months before I finally got my head above water. In any case, however tough it was, all I could do was study English vocabulary.

The words were not in the dictionary and my colleagues would not tell me what they meant. If I did not know them I would be mocked, so all I could do was find out their meanings myself and learn them. So I just had to plug away at learning English used in trading, foreign exchange and finance.

These are terms that you do not need unless you work in those fields, and it is perfectly natural that you do not know it. Nowadays, there is a test called TOEIC to gauge business English ability, and roughly 8,000 economic terms are said to appear in it. However, there are at least 30,000 or more economic terms that are in fact commonly used. So, if you specialize in work related to economics, you will forever be encountering specialized terms that you will need to know. All that you can do is treat such an occupation as a challenge, and study. You simply have to overcome it.

In fact, what I did was read things like English dictionaries and economics articles in English newspapers, underlining parts in red, and interpreting them the best I could. I would write down words and expressions that I did not understand and feverishly hunt down their meanings over the weekends. I kept a scrapbook of English newspaper articles and methodically looked up any words, phrases, or expressions that I did not know, and then compile them in folders or notebooks and study them.

When you do that, strangely enough, you will find that there is a limited number of these words. There is only a certain number of them. If you master them to some extent, you can use them. This is not a matter of whether or not you are clever, but simply whether or not you know the words. If you use English in your actual work, over the years you gradually pick up vocabulary on different occasions.

It simply depends on a person's character; some people are unable to endure a sense of inferiority unless they can understand something as soon as possible, while others can put up with the situation of not knowing and think nothing of it. I was the type who quickly developed a strong inferiority complex at not being able to do things. I made a lot of effort, thinking that somehow I had to catch up with the others. If you do that, you will find that you have mastered something before you realize it.

Words used differently in trading companies

What is more, in trading companies, words are sometimes used differently from how they are normally used. For example, there is the English word assignment. In Japan, this word means "homework" according to the English we learn at school. Your homework for the summer holidays is an "assignment." However, in trading companies, "assignment" is not used to mean homework.

One day a senior colleague asked me, "What are you going to do about your assignment?" I wondered, "Huh? My homework? That's a bit odd. What's he talking about? I clearly haven't got any homework," when in fact he meant my "allotted tasks." Assignment can also mean the block of work that is allocated or allotted to someone. In trading companies they just naturally use the English, not the Japanese, for this and say things like, "What are you going to do about your assignment?"

I was shocked to hear this word from a senior colleague who had graduated from some provincial university I had never even heard of, and I wondered if I had chosen the wrong career. Once you know a word, it's a trivial thing. But in a trading company, people laugh at someone who thinks the word assignment only means "homework" and does not understand that they are discussing what to do about their workload.

After joining the company, I was in a workplace where unknown words filled the air

The same thing sometimes happened with Japanese words, not just English ones. For example, a section manager about twenty years older than me suddenly said, "It's a five-zero day, so the roads are busy," and I wondered just what a "five-zero" day was. It was an expression I had not learned at school so I didn't know it. He said, "What? You don't know what a five-zero day is?!" and I have a bitter memory of being mocked.

The meaning of a five-zero day is not particularly difficult. It merely refers to a day that ends in a five or a zero, namely the 5th, 10th, 15th, 20th, 25th and 30th. The roads are busy on those days because they are often the deadlines for business transactions. There are more cars on the road on those days, so if you are scheduled to go somewhere you might be delayed in a traffic jam. You, therefore, have to factor this into your schedule.

However, I had not heard the expression before so I asked what a five-zero day was, and the response was, "What? You're a Tokyo University graduate and you don't know what a five-zero day is?!" I wanted to say that there are no classes at the University of Tokyo that teach such an expression, but that would have been showing disrespect towards my boss so I held my tongue.

"You don't even know that!" he said, and in fact it was true. I certainly didn't know such an old-fashioned expression. It was wrong of me not to know, because if you are working in the trading business you are expected to know this expression. So there are many business and trading terms that people such as students do not know, in Japanese as well as in English. I discovered many terms that I did not know related to things such as bills and contracts.

I remember how each time I encountered a word I did not know, it got me down. Even though I had been considered brilliant at the standard subjects at school, at work I encountered many words that I had definitely never seen before. Someone with a certain amount of experience in a company knows these words, but a new recruit does not, which makes things very hard for him. However, you cannot just suffer over the fact that you do not know. You must get on with your work and learn those words.

Whether a person will try and learn them or not probably depends on the individual, but if you do want to learn them, you have to study them for yourself. Nobody will teach you, so you have to expand your knowledge on your own by memorizing vocabulary or doing some reading. I remember doing this during my time at the trading company.

I had a hard time studying before entering university, but once I got in, I thought I did well in my academic studies. When I started work and came across words that were from an unfamiliar field, I had the experience of being completely incapable of doing my tasks. It felt like an incredibly long time before I could get my head around this. But after six months or so I could understand the words my colleagues were using.

When you are watching a historical drama series set in the provinces, for example, words you have never heard before fly back and forth, and it's hard to catch what people are saying. In exactly the same way, there were often times at work when unknown words were flying back and forth and I did not understand their meanings. Therefore, there were times when a new recruit like me could not communicate with section managers, and so I had to get colleagues who were two or three years my senior to "interpret." I was often called an idiot. I have had these sorts of experiences.

During my time at the trading company, all my mistakes roused me to action

During my time at the trading company, I was on the receiving end of a great many insults and criticisms, not just over the issue of vocabulary but also for mistakes in carrying out my work and procedures. I was even subjected to personal criticism. However, thinking about it now, I feel grateful for all of those things, as they served to rouse me into action.

Nobody is "Mr. Perfect" from the very beginning. What you do not know, you do not know. What you cannot do, you cannot do. However, if you do not try to learn what you do not know, you will never know it. If you do not make an effort to master what you cannot do, you will never be able to do it.

If you just give up and say, "I can't do it," you will not get any further. In that case, you are either labeled "incompetent" and are let go by the company, or you are a deadwood. Those are the only paths available to you. It is a question of whether or not you can overcome that. That is where you have to endure.

This is something that can be said particularly to young people who have just become working adults. When you go out into the world, you will encounter lots of words and ideas that you do not understand. Actually, this is something everyone experiences. Someone who experienced this will easily understand, but people experiencing it for the first time will be at a complete loss.

I also discovered that you need to learn things in advance, even out in the world. It is not enough for you to simply do the work you are being given now. You have to watch with interest, the work of your senior colleagues or bosses who are more than ten years older than you. You have to listen carefully to the words that they use on the phone or in conversations. Prepare yourself in advance and think, "This is the kind of work that I will be doing in a few years' time."

It is important to gather information as you learn, and to study things in advance. You need to think about whether you will be able to do that kind of work when you reach their position. This is what I learned at that time.

3. Keep on Challenging Yourself to Take on Unfamiliar Tasks

I abandoned everything and launched a religion without any funds

I have written elsewhere about the days just before I renounced the world and founded this religion, the moment I experienced the "conquering of the devil and attaining of enlightenment."* For me, the anguish I felt when leaving the company and setting up on my own was quite a major trial. I was being asked whether I was capable of making it on my own after I had abandoned all that I had accomplished through my efforts thus far.

Most of my work at the trading company had been in the finance department, where I spent quite a while in, so I knew a lot about financial issues such as how to draw up a financial plan. So, before establishing Happy Science, I had to draw up a rather bleak financial forecast, given the situation that I had almost no capital to fund it.

The high spirits from the heavenly world told me that people would soon come onto the scene to help me, but at the beginning there were no such people. When I started publishing spiritual messages, I got a lot

* See *Twiceborn* [New York: IRH Press, 2020] and *My Own Workbook of Life* (original title, published by Happy Science, available only in Japanese).

of letters from fans. But there were no concrete offers such as, "I will contribute this much, so please make use of it," or "I will contribute this much money."

I therefore lacked any firm foundations, but in the end I thought, "If I don't do it now, I'll never be able to," and I took the plunge and established Happy Science. I started out with no funds and gradually expanded our small organization.

Learning how to build a religion from the founders and histories of other religions

Although I can't remember them all now, I took on a huge number of challenges at that time. I devised many creative and ingenious ways in areas that were not noticed by people who joined us after we had grown into a big organization.

Earlier, I mentioned how hard it was when I came across a field that I did not study academically. After I established Happy Science, I experienced the difficulty of tackling unfamiliar tasks. There was nothing I could refer to when it came to creating a religion.

I had never been taught how to create a religion, and there was nowhere to learn this. So as I ran our religious group, I read many things that the founders of other religions wrote and the histories of religious organizations, and compared what each group had to say.

There was nothing written in those biographies and histories that was directly useful as a reference. But they did tell me things like how old the founders were when they did various things, so I looked at that while taking a "guess" at how to create a religion.

I would compare several writings while imagining, "At that time they must have done something roughly like this," or "They adopted this approach here," and I gleaned a general understanding of how a religion should probably be run. I studied in this way and created a religious organization myself.

Studying on my own, and establishing a publishing company and shojas

It was the same when I created IRH Press. Looking back, it seems almost laughable, but of course I had no experience of launching a publishing company, so it was incredibly difficult. Having worked at a trading company did not mean that I had any knowledge of how to create a publishing company.

But with the cooperation of a believer who was a printer, I was able to launch an interim publishing company. He promised me that he would publish books as our stand-in until IRH Press was established as an incorporated public company, then hand over all the rights and interests to us. However, when IRH Press actually became an incorporated public company, he started to rage against me because he didn't want to lose those rights and interests. It was a very tough situation because Happy Science could not acquire the rights to the books, even though I had written them.

At that time, one of our guiding spirits Gyōki* gave me this advice: "You cannot get other people to do things that you cannot do yourself." He told me, "It is wrong to get someone to run a publishing company even though you cannot do it yourself, and then just hope to reap the rewards. You have to make enough effort to build the publishing company yourself." After receiving this advice, I remember studying a lot on my own.

After that, as part of our main work as a religion, we constructed various buildings such as shojas. However, I had never learned how to construct a shoja, which is a facility for overnight seminar courses and so on, so I had to think it all out for myself. When I delegated this job to our staff members, everything they built looked like office buildings, so I worked hard to change this.

---

* Gyōki (668 - 749): Japanese Buddhist monk who was the first to be given the rank of *Daisōjō* (highest rank of monkhood in Buddhism).

Leveraging our accomplishments at Buddha's Truth cram school to establish an incorporated educational institution

Once we had grown as a religion, there was also the great endeavor of creating Happy Science Academy, an incorporated educational institution. Before creating the school, we ran our Buddha's Truth cram school, Success No. 1, as a trial for about ten years, and then used that as leverage to create our school.

When Success No. 1 was launched, I announced from the very start my aspiration to establish a school in the future. But I have to admit that immediately after the launch of Success No. 1, I was not confident in doing so.

I had no idea how to establish a school, but I realized that I could not establish a school without, at the very least, knowledge and information on what the children should study. So to begin with, we taught Buddha's Truth while also providing guidance that prepared elementary, junior high and high school students for their entrance exams. I expected that a path would eventually open up if we accumulated this knowledge and information. In fact, I was able to establish a school, just as I had initially hoped.

We are now trying to establish a university (scheduled to open in 2015). When I founded our religious organization, I thought it would be extremely difficult to open a university. Now, however, with "establishing a university" as my goal, I can think about what will be taught at the university and now I am able to produce a general outline of a curriculum. Since I have to be able to understand and talk about what will be at the core of this university, I am studying and preparing in my own way. I will have to entrust the operations to others. I have learned how to do this from past experience.

The launch of a political party with believers and staff who had no experience in politics

The same could be said about the Happiness Realization Party. We are still facing hardships and difficulties. I am not expecting to make a big achievement right away since it has only been a few years from its launch.

It would not be difficult for me to express various views like a commentator by writing books in the name of political reform and publishing them as an expression of my own views. If I studied subjects such as politics and the mass media, and wrote books on them, that would be the end of the story. We already have a publishing company, so if I published the books from there, it would be perfectly possible to publicize my opinions as a pundit.

However, I have launched a political party. It is very hard to launch one with only the help of believers and staff who have absolutely no experience in politics, and the past few years have been very difficult. But rather than simply publicizing my own opinions on politics, I have decided to launch a political organization. As we all study together and continuously undertake various activities as a group, what were simply my individual opinions are gradually becoming the opinions of a large organization.

The Happiness Realization Party is steadily growing as an organization and, in that sense, we are seeing a tremendous increase in its influence on society. I believe that someday it will probably become a force to pull Japan and the rest of the world forward.

I am thinking far into the future. I personally have goals that accord with that. However, if I were asked whether the current Happiness Realization Party actually has sufficient knowledge of political activities or political experience to be entrusted with governing Japan, I would have to say that in some respects it is not entirely adequate. Therefore, I believe that we will have to continue as we are now, studying together and accumulating knowledge and experience without any guidance. Given this, we must patiently endure failures, setbacks, criticisms and insults.

4. Never Compromise Your Strong Belief, and Keep on Trying

Do not fear failure and acquire the strength to endure criticism

Life is like that. If you fear failure, all you have to do is choose the easy path and merely focus on what you can do or what you are good at, and do nothing else. That is one choice in life. However, if you try to take on new challenges, you are always going to run into difficulties.

Success does not usually come instantly. You cannot achieve your goals without paying your dues. Until you get results, it is important to keep developing your mental strength and accumulating steady effort. What is more, you need the strength to endure criticism. Even when people say all kinds of abusive things about you or assail you, it is very important to overcome this and acquire the strength to withstand it.

People like professional politicians may have their own opinions. As elections draw closer, however, criticism from the opposition gets harsher and harsher, so they retract their opinions and start expressing themselves ambiguously. They only say things that they think are safe to say. In fact, they merely stick to the attitude, "Promise nothing. Reveal nothing. Commit to nothing."

We, the Happiness Realization Party, may still be classified as amateur politicians, but, from our point of view, the behavior or stance of such politicians is not the ideal form of politics. A trustworthy government should state clearly what needs to be done and make efforts to achieve what they have promised.

I do not believe that it is right for a democratic institution to speak in vague and ambiguous terms. Either that or say what is contrary to its own opinions and, once elected, become defiant and do something different. There are things that must not be compromised, no matter how much you are criticized. In that sense, it is very important never to compromise your beliefs.

If there is nothing wrong with your motives and goal, you must put up with hardships. Otherwise, you will never have any great success at anything, be it in the field of religion, politics, business or education.

Like a tortoise, keep moving forward, one step at a time

In the context of triumphing over trials, I believe that seriously tackling and overcoming as many difficulties as you can will lead you on a path to succeed in life. If you pray to God that you will not encounter any trials and ask only for a peaceful life, at the end of your days, you will probably feel regret for having dreams that were too small.

Rather than visualizing a paltry dream and being happy to say, "I achieved it 100%, I want to leave this world saying, "I didn't reach my goal, but I got halfway there. It's a shame but I will leave the rest to my successors." That is how I feel.

In that sense, you must all become stronger and develop the ability to stand up against any criticism. There are not all that many "weapons" that will help you fight them. You need the strength to endure patiently, like a tortoise that protects its body inside its shell. And even if the criticism continues, it is important to keep moving forward like a tortoise, one step at a time.

In other words, you need to accumulate steady efforts. Even though you may be mocked as an amateur, by continuing to work hard, you will be able to follow the path to becoming a professional before you know it.

It has been more than forty years now since I aspired to learn. If you keep going for more than forty years, anyone, whoever it may be, will achieve a level higher than average. You have to devote plenty of time to tackling what cannot be mastered in a short time with your ability, so it is important to keep moving forward like a tortoise. You need to make steady efforts.

Have the guts to return to the starting point and start again from scratch

Even if you fail and lose everything, it is important to have the guts to start again from scratch. Whenever I encounter various hardships or difficulties, I always try to return to my starting point. I, then, think back: "I had nothing before I started Happy Science. I had no followers, no funds, and nothing that would serve as capital. I did not have enough experience or information. I started fumbling for a way forward then, and now I have gotten this far."

If that is not enough, I go even further back and think: "I was born in a rural area and brought up like the average child. But realizing that I could blaze the path to advancement with just a pencil in hand, I became enthusiastic about learning and gradually earned recognition. Looking back over the time between then and now, a major factor in my success was that I did not stop moving forward."

I have tried my hand at many things. Had I consulted a hundred people before starting my religious work, all of them would probably have advised me to abandon such an impossible dream. I have actually completed a feat that a hundred people would no doubt have opposed. They would have opposed it, not because they were critical, but because they were truly concerned for me. I do have self-confidence from having accomplished this.

The great aspiration at the root of tenacious perseverance

Around ten years ago, I contracted a potentially fatal illness and thought that I had entered the final stage of my life. I remember that at that time, while in the hospital, I proofread *The Laws of Success*.* I wrote its Preface and Postscript, and completely ignoring the fact that I was ill, wrote in extremely confident prose.

At around the same time, I instructed Happy Science General Headquarters to produce an advertisement that commemorated the publication of my 400th book. At that time, I thought that writing 400 books was enough for a lifetime's work, and I remember telling the doctor, "I have given sufficient lectures and have written around 400 books, so maybe it is okay for me to die now."

However, although my works numbered around 400 books about ten years ago, as of mid-2013, they now number more than 1,400 if we include books published overseas and those published internally,   within Happy Science. Also, at that time, I had given just under 1,000 lectures but now that figure is over 2,000. In that way, I experienced for myself that precisely when people think the end has come, it is time to start anew.

When I started my missionary tour of our local branches in 2007, I thought, "These are probably my last lectures, so I want to meet all the members of our

* Jaico Publishing House

local branches at least once as a final farewell." But as I continued visiting the local branches, my body got stronger. I gradually gained strength and started to have more stamina than before. I could work so hard that I wondered what I had been doing up until then, so you never know what life will bring.

That kind of tenacious perseverance is important. It is rooted in having great aspirations and not giving up easily. That is what is needed.

Unite to multiply our power and accomplish great work

In this chapter I have focused mainly on my own experiences, though I feel a little embarrassed. I would like each individual believer and staff member in Happy Science to acquire knowledge, wisdom, experience and willpower, too, and to grow and develop. At the same time, Happy Science must start utilizing teamwork and accomplishing great work as an organization. That is our next challenge.

The work that can be done by a single individual is little. However, when many people join forces, they become capable of doing great work. The joining of people cannot simply be an "addition." If someone simply does the work that can be done by one person, then two such people will do the work of two people. If there are five, this number becomes five and if there are ten, perhaps they will produce the work of ten people, but that is not good enough. We must become capable of multiplying people's power to accomplish great feats.

It is my task from now on to lead Happy Science forward, so that we can do work with great additional values which will create a ripple effect and have more influence befitting our large organization. I believe that it is the mission of those who follow me to have that same goal and aspire to provide guidance for the world. In this chapter, I provided a brief outline on the theme "triumph over trials." I hope that it will be helpful.

CHAPTER THREE

Generating Virtue

~ Become Selfless and Live for Your Calling ~

Lecture given on April 19, 2013
at Happy Science General Headquarters
Tokyo, Japan

1. Take a Fresh Look at Yourself from a Wider Perspective

Teaching someone to be a person of virtue is not so easy

Recently I have been thinking a lot about virtue and would like to say something about that. This is because the year 2013 marked the 32nd anniversary of my Great Enlightenment and the 27th anniversary of the establishment of Happy Science. But I feel that I have not yet taught my disciples enough about virtue. The issue I must tackle now is whether or not I can skillfully express my thoughts regarding virtue.

People tend to think about their position or status solely within the group to which they belong. It is therefore difficult for them to think about how they appear from outside their own group, in the overall picture or from the perspective of people in other countries. It is very hard to see yourself in these sorts of ways.

Generally speaking, people tend to place themselves within a group of people with similar ways of thinking, abilities and talents as themselves. In other words, they try to think within the group that resembles their own ideas. They can hardly imagine the thoughts and feelings of people who are in a completely different circle.

It is not so easy to answer the question of what people can do to generate virtue. Since we opened the Happy Science Academy Junior and Senior High School, we started using the phrases "moral education" and "nurturing people of virtue." But if I am asked, "So, exactly what kind of education will cultivate virtue? What kind of a person is considered a person of virtue?" I am well aware that these questions are not so easy to answer.

The virtue of a homogeneous group may not be accepted by the world at large

A little while ago I received a report from our Student Division about the gatherings of new students who entered universities in 2013.

Some of the graduates from the Happy Science Academy Senior High School have entered universities that are regarded as elite in this world. These students were, of course, highly regarded and respected within the Happy Science Academy and were thought of as "people of virtue." However, when they entered universities that brought together elites from all over Japan and put themselves out there, apparently they found that it was not so easy to gain everyone's approval. To put it more plainly, they were ridiculed or criticized.

When students who graduated from the Happy Science Academy earnestly say what kind of person they are at their new universities or colleges and try to explain their beliefs or faith to others, they are met with harsh comments and sometimes get so depressed that they are damaged to some extent by negative spiritual influences.

These young people may have been sheltered and highly rated when they were at a school full of others who shared their faith. But if they go elsewhere else, they experience such unbelievable situations. Actually, these situations are nothing special for students who have never attended a school that is founded on faith. These occurrences are typical for students who go to ordinary, non-religious junior or senior high schools.

At public junior and senior high schools, students who declare that they have a faith are thought to be "unusual" and are generally treated coldly. They become aware that they must become wiser to survive. On the other hand, students who gathered together and spent years at a school that aims to create a religious elite have yet to build up resistance against harsh treatment. So, even though they do well during their time at school, once they leave for the outside world, they often experience rough times.

Therefore, we have to create some kind of culture or way of thinking that enables them to survive out in the world. If they try to take refuge in the Happy Science University simply because they cannot do well at other universities, it will be a problem. The same situation may well arise four years later when they leave university for the outside world.

So we should stop and think about whether what we call "virtue" within Happy Science is accepted as such by the world at large. Something naturally evaluated as positive by all the members of a homogeneous group is not always evaluated in the same way outside the group. We need to be aware of just why this happens.

The ability to take a fresh look at yourself from a wider perspective indicates the growth of virtue

As I mentioned earlier, in the end we need to seek our answer by thinking about the following: "How are we seen by people who belong to groups that are different from ours? How does society as a whole or the nation as a whole look at us? How are we seen from other countries? After all, are we capable of looking at ourselves from such a broad perspective?" I believe that, in a sense, becoming capable of taking a fresh look at yourself from a wider perspective actually indicates the growth of your virtue.

There are people in different fields in society who achieve various forms of success and get ahead in life. It is rather difficult to understand how others evaluate that. The president of a company can swagger around like an emperor in his own company when it expands. However, it is hard for him to know how he is rated by the outside world. You have to look at this objectively, though it is very difficult to do.

2. Make Efforts Not to Give in to the Laws of the Living World

The natural laws of the world of life seen in animals

Here, I will present the conclusion of this chapter in advance.

If we consider humans as beings that possess the attributes of an organism, living creature or animal, it is only natural that they will act for their own benefit. It is also natural to try to avoid anything that will put them at a disadvantage. It is perfectly natural that humans have this trait.

If you observe animals, this trait is obvious. Animals with large bodies or a very aggressive nature, such as lions, tigers, rhinos and crocodiles will indeed make the most of their characteristics of strength or the ability to defeat enemies. Their way of survival is based on the idea that a good offense is the best defense.

On the other hand, weak animals of prey such as rabbits, squirrels, mice, deer and zebras think about the best way to detect danger and flee. There is a proverb, "a wise rabbit digs three holes," which explains how rabbits think of ways to escape by having different hiding places. Rabbits have long ears to hear well, while animals with whiskers, such as cats, have them so that they can understand their surroundings, even in dark places such as under a floor or down a hole.

In this way, weak animals focus on how to protect themselves, while strong animals think about how to attack, capture their prey and put themselves in an advantageous position. Both of these tendencies exist in people's characters, too, though there are differences between individuals.

Also, there are people who fall somewhere between the two types, rather like foxes and raccoons, who make their way through society using deception. Seen in a positive light, this is wit. They may be cunning, but there are also people who are trying to survive by employing some kind of "wisdom." This is probably a natural law in the living world.

Religious leaders and revolutionaries take actions that go against the laws of nature

Historically, we can say that many people who were considered to "have virtue" often took actions that went against those laws of the living world. They do things that ordinary people would not.

In their actions is a greater wisdom than what ordinary people living on earth can conceive of. Within them, those who are aware of what will happen in the future will make their decisions and take actions based on that great wisdom, even if others do not understand at the time. Others find evil in what is being done in their region and era, and are determined never to give in to such evil. Refusing to submit to such values, they fight against them even if it results in their death. These types of people are particularly common among religious leaders and revolutionaries.

Sometimes we can find virtuous and respected people among those whose actions go against the laws of nature. Unfortunately, however, relatively few of them gain recognition while they are alive. Many of them are recognized some time after their death, and there are some who never are.

It's not easy for you to be content with being evaluated hundreds of years later when you live in this world as a human being, earn a living, have a job and a family to look after. While you are still alive you have to be appreciated by your family, colleagues and bosses. This is more important for most people, and those who are content with being evaluated centuries later or maybe a thousand years in the future are generally labeled dreamers. So this issue is extremely difficult.

MacArthur saw "a living god" in Emperor Shōwa

I will talk about these things in a way that is easy to understand, and provide a number of examples. One leader, for example, would be Emperor Shōwa of Japan.

It is said that when MacArthur* arrived in Japan as the Supreme Commander of the occupation forces, he was amazed when Emperor Shōwa** came in person to GHQ (General Headquarters of the Supreme Commander for the Allied Powers) and said, "I am not concerned with my own fate. I do not mind if I am executed, but I would like you to provide food for my people and help them." I'm not sure whether this story is an exaggeration or not.

It is said that MacArthur was stunned by Emperor Shōwa's coming to GHQ. It is because once he came into GHQ on his own, there was a strong possibility that he would be executed. Apparently, MacArthur said something along the lines of, "I have seen a living god," although that might be an overstatement.

Moreover, after losing the war, Emperor Shōwa went on an imperial tour of the country and traveled throughout Japan with practically no security to guard him. In fact, not a single terrorist attack or riot occurred. The occupation forces were amazed by this. During the war, the American army considered Japan to be the

* General Douglas MacArthur (1880 - 1964): Played a prominent role in the Pacific War during World War II.

** Emperor Shōwa (1901 - 1989): 124th Emperor of Japan. His name was Hirohito. Reigned from 1926 to 1989. He prayed and watched over the development of Japan as a symbolic emperor after Japan's defeat in World War II (Great East Asia War).

equivalent of a fascist state and a very evil nation. They assumed that if the Emperor were to appear before the masses, it would be strongly likely for him to be lynched and killed. They assumed that was the kind of person an emperor was, but Emperor Shōwa undertook an imperial tour around the entire country, and apparently was not attacked even once. He was not heavily guarded by the police, either.

For example, Shōichi Watanabe* writes about this in one of his books. Watanabe spent his youth in Yamagata Prefecture and at the time of Japan's defeat he was around fifteen years old. Then he witnessed Emperor Shōwa's visit to Yamagata. He writes, "We had been playing on the embankment and when Emperor Shōwa arrived we rushed to greet him. His Majesty had no guards with him." Even though he had no security, Emperor Shōwa was not attacked.

When the GHQ saw this situation, they gained the impression that Emperor Shōwa was not a dictator like Hitler or Mussolini. Mussolini met a terrible death. There is a photograph of him strung up after being killed by the masses, so he met a terrible end. Hitler ended up committing suicide. They met such deaths. On the contrary, Emperor Shōwa survived the end of

* Shōichi Watanabe (1930 -): Japanese scholar of the English language, and critic. Professor emeritus at Sophia University. Aside from his expertise in the English language, he is also giving many speeches as a conservative speaker.

the war and made efforts to create Japan's prosperity for some decades after that. I presume that the GHQ saw Emperor Shōwa as being quite extraordinary, and probably sensed something about him that was not of this world.

It seems that Emperor Shōwa himself felt a tremendously heavy responsibility for the way in which so many young people hurled themselves at the enemy in the last war, and died shouting, "*Banzai*! (Long live the Emperor!)" for example, in *kamikaze* units. He probably was not relieved from that yoke, or burden, after the war. I think that he was not free of it his whole life. Nevertheless, I assume that he gradually regained a peace of mind from the prosperity that the country later enjoyed.

The pitiful end of Saddam Hussein, dragged from a hole in the ground

I'm not sure whether or not he should even be compared with Emperor Shōwa – in the case of Iraq's Saddam Hussein, I got the impression that we were shown something that we did not really want to see. After all that boasting about taking on even America, he was captured hiding like a rat in a hole in the ground on the outskirts of his hometown of Tikrit. After his arrest, footage of him being dragged out of his hiding place was shown on television. Being captured like that was rather deplorable; it would be inconceivable in Japan.

In his case, there was an inconsistency between his public display and his inner self. He roared like a lion for show, but in point of fact scurried away like a rat. Whereas in Japan, after the war, the prime minister and people of ministerial rank tried to commit suicide, and some of them succeeded in doing so. There were many who tried to commit suicide and dispose of themselves in that way, rather than fall into the hands of the occupation forces. There is something unforgettable about Saddam Hussein's end, and no one would support him for hiding in such a way.

Aum's Asahara, hiding in a secret room pretending to be a madman

Many people in the Japanese mass media felt that they had seen the scene of Saddam Hussein's arrest before. I think it was probably because they were recalling the following events.

In the Aum Incident of 1995, the riot police raided a Japanese cult Aum's* facilities known as Satyam in

---

* Aum Shinrikyo is the organization responsible for the 1995 sarin gas attack in the Tokyo subways.

Kamikuishiki village (as it was known then), in Yamanashi Prefecture. But, no matter how hard they searched, they could not find the founder, Asahara. Eventually, they discovered that Asahara had been hiding for hours in a secret room built into the ceiling.

The riot police knocked on the walls of the building, and when they found a place where it made a different sound, they guessed something was there. When they removed the wall, they found someone hiding. They asked, "Are you Asahara?" and he answered, "Yes, I am." So his hiding place was revealed and he was captured. TV commentators said something like, "Even people like us who aren't believers have been disappointed by this. We expected him to be a little more imposing."

Having seen that, the scenes of Saddam Hussein's capture probably resembled the scenes of Asahara's. Asahara had built a secret room in advance in the Satyam so he could hide there if something happen. Outwardly, he was aggressive and made threats such as, "In order to save humankind, we will spread sarin gas from helicopters in the skies above Tokyo and massacre its citizens," while on the other hand, he prepared a place to hide away and protect himself like Lupin III* in order to survive. What can we say about such contradictions?

---

* *Lupin III* is a famous Japanese comic book series written by Monkey Punch about the escapades of master thief Lupin III.

What is more, he continues to play the madman even after he was captured and put into detention, as well as at his trials. I do not know if he really has gone mad, but perhaps he actually did while he was frantically acting like a madman to avoid execution. I am not so sure about all that, but I could see that he was putting on various acts so he could escape the death sentence.

It is manful and proper for a religious leader to continue proclaiming his beliefs confidently up to his death, even if they are mistaken. Even if they are wrong, if he were to say, "I did it out of my belief. I believed that the voice of God I heard was true and I carried out what it said," that would be reasonable for a religious leader. I was disappointed that he seemed to be putting on various acts to protect himself.

3. A Simple Way to See Through People

You can understand a person's true nature when they experience extreme highs and lows

I have mentioned several times in the past that if you want to know a person's true nature, an easy method would be to raise and lower his status alternately, and observe the attitude in both cases. You can get a pretty good idea of what a person is like by promoting him to the very top or demoting him to the very bottom, having him experience both extremes.* You really can understand people very easily using this method.

Of course, very few people get angry when they move up in rank. They generally become cheerful and very loyal. They sometimes become mild, kind and generous to others, giving the impression that they have gained in virtue. However, in the course of the past twenty years or so, I have unfortunately seen many people whose attitude suddenly changed when they were demoted.

There is nothing particularly unusual about people becoming devoted and pious when they are promoted. But not many people can retain those qualities when they are demoted. I have seen people who experienced both promotion and demotion, then lost devotion or

---

* See *An Unshakeable Mind*, Lantern Books, and other writings.

faith, eventually drifted away from Happy Science. This is so, even if they had the experience of being in top management. They quit as a staff member or left the organization completely.

Also, some people are making some kind of an attack against Happy Science after they leave us. I can understand how they feel, but they cannot claim to have virtue. As soon as they can no longer make a living, feel that their reputation was damaged or were demoted, they suddenly do a 180 degree turn. They turn away from the faith which they had believed in up until then and even recommended to others. I cannot help but get the impression that these people have no virtue. I find it disappointing when they reveal such traits.

Though too simple a method of evaluation, if you observe a person both when he is promoted and when he is demoted, you will get a fairly good idea of his true nature. Decent people unceasingly do what needs to be done whether their status rises or falls because they themselves are no different, whatever their position may be. On the other hand, people who make decisions based on their own interests unfortunately fall into the category of mediocrity. Nonetheless, they may seem like great people at one time.

In the case of business people there is only a thin line between "hero" and "villain"

Apart from religious faith, there are a number of what could be called quasi-faiths in this world. These are based on worldly evaluations. Some people have a kind of faith in academic background or in medical school. There is also a quasi-faith in worldly advancement such as being promoted to a position like company president or managing director, or quasi-faith in a company name or a prestigious brand. There are various objects of worship, such as "where you work" or "how much money you earn."

These are not really the same as objects of faith, but I presume that many people feel that attaining some degree of worldly standing that everyone wants is an act of quasi-faith. There are many situations in society where people feel that the higher they rise, the more others venerate them with these kinds of worldly evaluations.

However, the day will eventually come when these people, too, have to leave their jobs. Even a company president resigns his or her position; even a rich person sometimes runs out of money. The question is whether or not their reputation will still hold at that time.

In the case of business people in particular, there is only a thin line between a hero and a villain. In the case of new businesses, for example, just when you think they are a huge success, the owner sometimes ends up behind bars. So it can be very hard to evaluate such people accurately. Other businesses may be doing similar things, and there is a very small gap between ending up on the inside or outside, and I get the feeling that virtue does to a certain extent play a role in that.

In our teachings, we have something called "the Three Happinesses (happiness saving, happiness sharing and happiness planting)." If the people in new businesses who are successful become frugal with their good fortune as taught in the teachings, and feel to a greater or less extent that they want to utilize their good fortune for the sake of others, they will be envied less and less by other people. However, that may be an unusual way of thinking and people don't seem to understand it.

A Japanese businessman, who used to be one of the standard-bearers of new businesses, once used the expression "there is nothing that money can't buy" as the blurb for his book. It might have been the editorial staff who put it on the cover. But it enraged the Public Prosecutor's Office and caused the prosecutors to think, "That's unforgivable. We're going to nail him." In some ways, the prosecutors were incited by those words, "There is nothing that money can't buy." It's unclear whether the man actually said those words himself, but in the end he was arrested.

The more you succeed, the greater you need to develop a certain degree of social intelligence. This includes a self-sacrificing attitude, as well as the wish to multiply other people's happiness and fortune.

Transcend likes and dislikes, and evaluate others with an impartial and egoless attitude

The higher your position becomes, the greater the influence you have on other people's lives; thus you must be as impartial and egoless as possible. Of course, humans have likes and dislikes, and there will be types of people that you like and types that you don't. That is natural, but you need to make an effort to go beyond your personal likes and dislikes, and establish an impartial attitude. If you make an effort with that sort of a mindset, you will gradually become more impartial and egoless.

There may be types of people you like and do not like from past experiences. However, you have to consider, for instance, whether a person is necessary or not, is an asset or not, or is useful or not from the perspective of your company, organization or country. You then have to make a judgment and choose between two conclusions: "We must keep that person on board and protect him or her" or "That person is becoming a bad influence and has to be removed."

The higher your rank, the more important it is to have a sense of impartiality and an attitude of verifying whether a person is right for a certain job. In that sense, even though you may actually have a gentle personality, you also need to have a certain degree of sternness. That rigor is necessary to fulfill your duties.

4. Be Aware of Yourself as a Public Figure as Befits Your Position

Yamaori's second treatise pointed out the importance of the Imperial family's official duties

Recently, a Japanese religious scholar, Tetsuo Yamaori, published his treatise, "Please Abdicate, Crown Prince" in the monthly magazine, *Shincho 45* (March 2013 issue). After that, we published a book that contained spiritual messages from the guardian spirits of both the Crown Prince and Yamaori.* But before it was published, Yamaori's second treatise, "The Form that Imperial Succession Should Take," appeared in the May 2013 issue of *Shincho 45*. I was still proofreading my book, so Yamaori's second treatise appeared before my book was published.

In his second treatise, Yamaori slightly fudged a few details and wrote a lot about matters that have absolutely nothing to do with the question of the Japanese Imperial family, such as the monarchical system in Europe. However, there was a passage about the main issue of imperial succession in which he wrote about the *mogari* ceremony.

---

* *Spiritual Interview with Guardian Spirits: Questioning the Crown Prince about His Self-Awareness as the Next Emperor* (tentative title), IRH Press Co., Ltd., available only in Japanese.

When an emperor passes away, the next emperor is immediately recognized and after a few hours people cheer, "Long live the Emperor!" At that time, the Imperial family carries out the tradition known as *mogari*. When the previous emperor had passed away, there was a rather long interval, around forty-five days, before his body was interred. During that time, the new emperor would sleep next to the body of the previous emperor to receive his spiritual power. In Japanese Shinto, this ceremony is called *mogari*. This was alluded to in the spiritual messages from Princess Masako's guardian spirit, which we published in 2012.* I get the feeling that this book may have given Yamaori some hints for his treatise.

To put it bluntly, this is a traditional Japanese Shinto religious ritual, and I presume that after a fashion Yamaori is asking whether Princess Masako understands that. In short, he seems to think that Princess Masako is simply unable to understand this religious act that exists within the imperial system. He seems to be indirectly criticizing her for that. That is the impression I got.

Incidentally, Princess Masako did not attend a garden party held on April 18, 2013 at the Akasaka Imperial Gardens in Tokyo. One reason was that Princess

---

* See *Praying for the Future of the Imperial Family* (tentative title), IRH Press Co., Ltd., available only in Japanese.

Masako is not really accustomed to garden parties since as many as 2,000 people gather there. But she went to the coronation of the new king held in the Netherlands. It is quite strange that she could go to the Netherlands though she could not attend the garden party in Japan.

Princess Masako could go to the Netherlands where she had been to before in connection with her father's work, but was unable to go to the Akasaka Imperial Gardens. Yamaori was probably irritated by that fact. To him it seems that she may be acting according to her own likings rather than doing her job. Perhaps he feels that she may not understand just what the official duties of the Imperial family are or how important they are, and that she may choose whether to attend events or not according to her personal preferences, just like a private individual working for an ordinary company. This is what he is sharply questioning.

Moreover, he is questioning whether the Crown Prince is aware of the issues, given that he cannot properly explain their official duties or persuade her. That is the impression I got.

I think it was after I had finished proofreading that book in mid-April 2013 that Prime Minister Abe's guardian spirit came to visit me three days in a row. I was not quite sure what was worrying him, but at that time the North Korean situation was a major problem.

A certain weekly magazine feels that Ryuho Okawa prioritizes official duties

In fact, in addition to the spiritual messages recorded in that book, Yamaori's guardian spirit later paid me a visit and we spoke for quite a long time, during which he said things slightly more appropriate to a religious scholar than he did when we recorded his spiritual message. Furthermore, he referred to my situation and half-apologetically mentioned that the mass media in some ways understands a bit more than I thought.

He also said about Shinchosha Publishing, "They have done a great deal of study in the process of attacking Happy Science. They try to attack Ryuho Okawa and see what happens, and try to attack the Imperial family and see what happens. Then they compare the two and evaluate them.

"As for Ryuho Okawa, usually when they attack somebody that strongly together with Bunshun magazine, the organization will collapse, or the leader will give up his vocation or some incident will occur and bring ruin, but Ryuho Okawa didn't give up his vocation. He just kept going, persistently maintaining his attitude that he would not give up his official duties, and didn't change one bit.

"If a religious man divorces his wife whom he had been married to for more than twenty years and had five children with, he would usually be attacked as socially unacceptable. Someone like this would be unable to endure such attacks. He would become anguished, unstable and would crumble. He would either be unable to continue his work, or some kind of incident would occur and ruin his religious organization. But Ryuho Okawa did not give up his vocation and his disciples did not leave him. He kept going just as before, with no change of policy. When the mass media saw that, no matter what they said, they became well aware that Ryuho Okawa's attitude of putting his official duties first hadn't wavered." That was what he said.

He also said, "By comparison, the Crown Prince may be giving slightly too much priority to personal matters. Thinking that, in some ways the media is viewing the Imperial family in a harsher light. The mass media is actually doing a comparison of the two." His comments sound rather strange and dodgy to me, but that is what he said.

Finally he said, "In effect, by not compromising his work and carrying through with it, Ryuho Okawa put himself on par with the four great saints." I do not know whether that was intended as a compliment or not.

He said, "The four great saints – Shakyamuni Buddha, Jesus Christ, Confucius and Socrates – all had a broken family life. In general, the family lives of saints are a mess. That is what saints are like. Of course they do have the ideal of treasuring the family and gradually expanding social units from society to a nation to create a utopia, but those are teachings for the masses. Usually the family lives of the saints are a mess. This is because saints must face trials that would usually never happen to normal people, and they have to fight such temptations. That is why it inevitably happens. Thus, Ryuho Okawa is on a par with the four saints." He praised me in this slightly suspicious way.

I do not know whether that was a good thing or whether it was a trap. He just praised me to the skies in the hope of escaping attack. In any case, he said that the people who write weekly magazines are gradually coming to understand my stance. Certainly, I agree to some extent that the media is changing slightly.

A public figure must disregard personal matters in accord with his or her position

Certainly, there are many people who believe in me and follow me. I could distort the messages in any way if I were fabricating these teachings for some kind of swindle. I could also distort the messages if I were doing this just for fame, status or money, or out of business greed. However, I do what I believe is the Truth and I cannot betray those who follow me. This is my principle so I do not change my course one little bit. That is why my lectures, which are often broadcast on TV overseas, have recently been shown a little on Japanese TV channels.

Yamaori's guardian spirit also had this to say: "When you launched your political party (The Happiness Realization Party) before the 2009 House of Representatives election, what you insisted on probably sounded very strange to people in general. Even though four years have passed, the critical situation of this country has not changed and the issues you viewed as problems have not yet been solved. However, what you said four years ago served Japan, preparing it more or less for a possible crisis. People now feel that what you say is not wrong. They have come to understand that what you are saying is right and that you do not budge on what you think is right."

The experience of becoming more of a public figure as you rise in position is not very common and is extremely hard to do. There is no one to teach you how to do it, nor is there a textbook on it, so you have to judge for yourself. Nevertheless, there is always an aspect to it of having to eliminate your own personal concerns.

The determination to exert your full potential will strengthen your power to push away any burden

I love my five children. Since I cherish them all, of course I do not feel animosity towards my ex-wife, who was with me for more than twenty years and bore me five children.

After I nearly died in 2004, I felt that I would always be prepared to die in their place. Even though I felt this way, it would have been unforgivable. This is because many people are contributing to the Happy Science organization, believing that this is their calling. According to accepted medical knowledge, it would not have been at all strange if I had died at that time. I was told that the probability of my dying within a year was greater than 80%. After that, I was told that I would definitely die within the next five years.

However, about ten years have passed since then and I'm still alive. And not only that, I am doing ten or twenty times the work I used to do. Accepted medical knowledge did not apply, which proves the merit of religion. I became even more of a religious leader.

I completely overturned accepted medical knowledge. One of the reasons I could do that was because paradoxically I thought I had to exert my full potential to leave behind no regrets. That is, if I only had a short time left to live. Having determined this led me to feel an even greater surge of zeal, passion and the will to act. While I was taking action, my power strengthened to push back the burden weighing on me.

In the meantime, my way of looking at the world and the country changed, and my sense of responsibility for them also changed. I came to feel a sense of responsibility even towards things I was not directly involved with.

There are actually no textbooks on how to balance public and private life. I feel I have to make some judgments on such matters. Of course, being born into this world as a human, there may be some mistakes in my thinking or actions. I cannot say that there are no mistakes. But at the very least I have never wavered in my attitude of adhering to the things that I deemed to be right and to be the Truth, after giving them some serious thought.

How to view Keigo Higashino's "Galileo" series

The detective stories by Keigo Higashino featuring a brilliant physicist are very popular in Japan and have been made into TV series and movies. The brilliant physicist featured in them thinks in the following way: "I do not believe in such an illogical thing as spirits. Such mysterious things and supernatural phenomena do not really exist. Things that cannot be explained by physics are completely impossible." That TV drama is highly rated as being rather interesting and is quite popular; I, myself, watch it as well.

It's fine as long as it keeps its conclusions within the limited world of physics. However, it is a fact that worlds other than the world of physics exist. It is fine to say, "This is so in the world of physics" but since they do not know about worlds other than that of physics, they should be careful of what they say.

The new TV series was filmed in 2013, and the first episode was a battle between the master of a religion and the physicist. The master of a certain religion sent thought waves in the form of "transmitted thoughts" but in fact, what he did was use a type of equipment to send out microwaves, warm the body and induce sensations of heat. While watching this, I thought that it was a really inconvenient drama for religious people.

Masaharu Fukuyama, who stars as the brilliant physicist, was also very popular in his role as Ryōma Sakamoto in the NHK historical drama "Ryōma-den (The Biography of Ryōma)." I do not think badly of him, or I should say he is the type of person whom I feel is very hard to criticize. But I would be troubled if materialism and atheism became popular.

At Happy Science, we conducted "remote viewings" to observe Nessie clairvoyantly as well as spiritually searched the other side of the moon.* The brilliant physicist in the Galileo series would deem such things impossible and as a physicist would no doubt want to launch into some clarification. So what Happy Science

---

* See *Remote Viewing: Does Nessie Exist?* (tentative title), IRH Press Co., Ltd, available only in Japanese, *Remote Viewing: The Dark Side of the Moon* (tentative title), March 13, 2012, available only in Japanese.

is doing is the complete opposite. However, we are just doing what needs to be done, even if outsiders judge our work in such a way.

It is possible to defend Higashino. I do not think that he is a complete materialist. In some of his works, he depicts scenes such as the split personality phenomenon where souls switch places. I understand that he has apparently studied quite a lot about paranormal phenomena. Apparently he is working very hard, researching what is fake and what is real at the boundaries of paranormal phenomena, so I am not completely rejecting Higashino. Nevertheless, I feel that this world can be very rigid.

I am continuing to publish books for readers a thousand years from now

Incidentally, when I hear that Haruki Murakami's new book of 2013 sold a million copies in one week, I am slightly tempted to summon the president of IRH Press. I want to ask him just what he is doing. If a million copies of Murakami's book are being sold in one week, I wonder just how high the sales will go in a year? So I thought, "I am sweating away producing a huge number of books and it really is quite hard work. Should I summon the president of IRH Press and give him a piece of my mind?"

However, the people around me say, "No, Mr. Murakami's works are short-lived. Before long they will be forgotten and will have vanished into oblivion. But Master Okawa's works will still be read a thousand years from now." Then I think, "I guess so. If people are going to be reading them a thousand years from now, then I must keep on working."

Even though I keep on producing books, my readers cannot get through them very quickly, so there is a tendency for it to be more difficult to boost sales the more I write. However, when I consider that I am leaving them behind for posterity, it makes me feel that I have to write them while I can. So, I must not adopt the approach of using gimmicks to sell many books. Accordingly, I will not stop working diligently.

5. The Four Great Saints Who Demonstrated to Humankind What Virtue Is

The way you embrace self-contradictory issues will give birth to virtue

I have so far spoken about various subjects related to virtue. Here, I will reiterate these in a different order.

For virtue to be born, there of course needs to be a person with some degree of greatness. Indeed, virtue is generated in a person who leads a life that is different from the ordinary way based on the usual biological reactions. For example, Shōin Yoshida,* the forerunner of the Meiji Restoration in the 19th century, is one such person. He most definitely had a different way of thinking from that of ordinary people. He had that quality. This is one instance in which virtue was born.

To put it more simply, when virtue is generated a person is always faced with some kind of paradoxical situation where opposing values or logics clash. When

---

* Shōin Yoshida (1830-1859): Born in the Chōshū region of Japan. He was a political activist and a teacher of military tactics and *Yōmeigaku* (Yangming philosophy) in the closing days of the Tokugawa Shogunate. Educating students in Shōka Sonjuku private school, he produced many competent leaders, and became the driving force of the Meiji Restoration. He was executed at the age of 29. He is an incarnation of *Amaterasu-Ō-Mikami,* a central figure of the Japanese gods.

virtue is generated, there is always a person who is able to embrace and accept both sides. It is extremely difficult to accept opposing values. So if someone is able to do that, it will create virtue for humans.

For example, in the case of Emperor Shōwa, it would be perfectly natural as a human being to think, "If I go to GHQ and give myself up, I might be killed." But there is also another feeling, "I want to save the people." These are mutually exclusive alternatives, so they have to be made compatible.

Another example is in work. Work must be done with precision and detail, but at the same time there must also be an overview. This is difficult as well. A prime minister has to look at the details of work, but at the same time he must look at the big picture, too. Being able to grasp contemporary trends is also important. A person may have learned much from his teachers about how to interpret the law. But when times change, he must make fresh decisions about how it should be regarded then. At that time, forces that criticize and oppose him will, of course, emerge. In the midst of that, how the decisions are made is very important.

In this way, there are many paradoxical situations and how you have embraced conflicting issues will determine whether or not you will generate virtue.

Virtue as seen in Socrates, Shakyamuni Buddha and Confucius

Socrates is another example of a man of virtue. He was sentenced to death. He had a wife and children, his disciples tried to help him, even his jailer tried to get him to escape, but he would not flee. Saying, "Bad laws are also laws," he drank a cup of wine poisoned with hemlock and died.

Socrates practiced the logic, "Sometimes it is more sacred to die for the Truth than to live" by taking this extremely paradoxical action. This is logic that the ordinary human being will find very hard to accept.

The same holds true of Shakyamuni Buddha. He abandoned his family and the Shakya clan. As a result, the Shakya clan died out. However, the Buddha practiced austerities in the mountains and forests to develop the new teachings now known as Buddhism, and he eventually became a religious leader.

Seen through modern eyes, or from the perspective of contemporary tabloids, what the Buddha did would surely provoke criticism. He would definitely be the target of criticisms such as "He gave up his position and left home, even though he was the sole heir. What will happen to the people he left behind?" Whichever way you look at it, he would surely be attacked as "an irresponsible man." However, his actions were necessary for the grand teachings of Buddhism to be left behind for posterity.

Confucius is yet another example. He preached virtues such as "courtesy," "wisdom," "trust," "righteousness" and "courage" with all his might, and is said to have had 3,000 disciples. But he, himself, just could not get a government position. He did once hold a position similar to the Minister of Justice in his homeland (the State of Lu) for a short time. But after that he wandered throughout the country looking for government work, only to be refused everywhere he went. So he continued his wanderings without finding employment.

The disciples of Confucius entered government service on the strength of his recommendations and some of them even became state ministers. In some ways, Confucius may have become famous through his disciples who rose to greatness.

Although Confucius was only one thinker from the Hundred Schools of Thought, the greatness of his thought and his influence over time have gradually increased over one or two thousand years. In his own day, there were undoubtedly very many people who were more eminent than him, for example kings and cabinet ministers. However, history surely evaluated things differently.

To fulfill his mission, Jesus entered Jerusalem prepared for death

Jesus Christ is an extreme case. His death is not comprehensible if we look at it using worldly logic. Before going to Jerusalem, he told his disciples, "I will enter Jerusalem but before long I will be crucified. However, I will be resurrected after three days." The disciples did not understand the meaning of what he was saying. They probably felt, "I feel sorry for the Master, but maybe he has gone a little crazy."

If he was going to be crucified for going into Jerusalem, all he had to do was not go. That is a truly logical decision. It is like Genzui Kusaka, a prominent 19th century Japanese samurai, pleading with his teacher Shoin Yoshida, "Please abandon that plan!" So the logical decision would be not to enter Jerusalem, and if he was supposed to be crucified he needed to flee. However, Jesus entered Jerusalem with the attitude that he must go there as it was his mission to do so.

Prior to this, Jesus said many "grandiose" things such as, "Even if the temple is destroyed, I will rebuild it in three days." So some people were wondering what kind of a miracle would occur. But Jesus was easily arrested, whipped, made to wear a crown of thorns and forced to climb the hill of Golgotha. Although he was made to carry his own cross, he could not hold it and collapsed, so someone else helped him climb the hill.

Then he was easily crucified, and died. A lot of people were very disappointed by this, "What? There was no miracle? No angels came to save him?!" As a result, his group straightaway fell into a state of devastation.

There are arguments about the meaning of Jesus' last words: "Eli, eli, lema sabachthani." In an early collection of our spiritual messages, Jesus says that he was calling out the names of angels: "Elijah, Elijah, Raphael, Raphael." However, a certain writer of the Gospels translates it as, "My God, my God, why hast Thou forsaken me?" That was probably the most acceptable interpretation that the people of the day could think of.

Although Jesus had lived as the only son of God, he was finally crucified. So people would feel that it was understandable if Jesus had said, "My God, my God, why hast Thou forsaken me?" That was the common feeling at that time, and even his disciples had that attitude, similar to the thinking of present-day tabloids.

The Unification Church of Sun Myung Moon took advantage of this weak point in Jesus' teachings

The person who took advantage of this weak point was Sun Myung Moon, the founder of the Unification Church. Based upon the Gospels, he said that it was inconceivable for the only son of God, born as the Messiah, to have said, "My God, my God, why hast

Thou forsaken me?" before his death. He says, "Thus, this Christ is a false Christ. This is a fake Christ, a sham. I, myself, am the real one. I, Sun Myung Moon, am the true Christ, who was born to save the world."

So, Sun Myung Moon adroitly took advantage of the inconsistencies in the Bible, proclaimed that he was the reincarnation of Christ and established the Unification Church. To put it simply, he took an unerring aim at a weak point in the Bible where Jesus' words had been interpreted according to what was commonly accepted, turned the teachings upside down and organized a new religion. That new religion is now the Vatican's vast enemy. He clearly took advantage of this weak point, or quickly picked up the points that would seem to be "wrong" from the common perspective of the tabloids.

And it is the religious people who are most easily deceived by that. They think, "Well, yes, it is strange that Jesus should say something like that. So, the Bible was wrong and this Jesus was not the Messiah. That is why Judaism did not perish but still exists today, and why the Jews do not believe in Christianity. I see, so it is this new person who is the Messiah." Religious people are rather nice people, and in some ways easily duped like this.

This kind of logic can be constructed, and that is why books like the Bible are in a sense very hard to interpret.

6. To Become a Person of Virtue

Virtue is revealed in personal episodes and in your real self as a human being

So, what else is needed to become a person of virtue in this world? It is not only religious people who possess virtue. There are also political leaders and revolutionaries who have virtue.

In the case of revolutionaries, there are some who really seem to be devils, as well as some who take action infused with a sacred mission. Both types of people fight, so in some ways it is not easy to judge in this world whether or not they possess virtue.

But surprisingly, this can be judged by looking at their personal lives and their real selves as human beings. You can tell what kind of person someone is from various episodes or from their interactions with other people. So you should give such matters serious attention.

To return to the treatise by Yamaori that I mentioned earlier (Section 4), he wrote about General Nogi,* who sacrificed himself for Emperor Meiji.** He

---

* Maresuke Nogi (1849 - 1912): General and an educator during the Meiji period. As Army General, he fought the Russo-Japanese War and served as the head of Gakushuin school after the war. Out of his desire not to outlive his master, he committed suicide on the day of Emperor Meiji's funeral.

** Emperor Meiji (1852 - 1912): 122nd Emperor of Japan. His name was Mutsuhito. Reigned from 1867 to 1912. He led the new Meiji government the way toward the development of modern Japan, as well as wealth and military growth.

wrote that General Nogi stayed beside the Emperor's corpse, watching over it throughout the entire religious ceremony, from start to finish, and when the funeral was over he followed him into death.

As I anticipated in *Spiritual Interview with Guardian Spirits: Questioning the Crown Prince About His Self-Awareness as the Next Emperor* (tentative title),* as a religious scholar, Yamaori probably intends to remonstrate with the next emperor and leave this world to follow the current Emperor into death. To put it bluntly, I perceive that he probably aspires to commit suicide.

There are various kinds of behavior. But to judge whether or not an act is truly virtuous requires historical verification. A person's true intentions also greatly influence this.

As a leader, do you have the power to control yourself?

What I want to say is this: generally speaking, virtue can be seen in someone who embodies two different vectors that are hard to reconcile in this world. Take Takamori Saigō,** for example. He was a prominent figure who overthrew the shogunate, established the

---

* IRH Press Co., Ltd, available only in Japanese.

** Takamori Saigō (1828 - 1877): Samurai and politician during the Bakumatsu period and the early Meiji period, who was from Satsuma. Successfully formed the Satsuma-Chōshū Alliance, and led the Edo Castle to surrender without bloodshed. He served as Army General in the Meiji government.

Meiji government in 19th century Japan and became a military general. Although he was a leading figure of the Meiji Restoration, he was indifferent to money and social status. People sense virtue in such a person.

Another example is Ryōma Sakamoto.* He played a leading role behind the scenes in the Satsuma-Chōshū alliance** during the Meiji Restoration. If this alliance had not been formed, the Meiji era would never have begun, and we would probably not be enjoying this era of peace now. Ryōma Sakamoto's efforts to forge an alliance between Satsuma and Chōshū are in fact one reason why modern Japan has come into being.

Ryōma experienced the restoration of imperial rule. At that time, he wrote "A Draft of Positions in the New Government" but his own name was not on it. When other people asked him why, apparently he responded, "When my work is finished, I want to take a ship and head overseas, I want to try my hand at foreign trade." He did

* Ryōma Sakamoto (1835 - 1867): A patriot during the Bakumatsu period, who was from Tosa. Under the influence of Kaishū Katsu, he mediated the Satsuma-Chōshū Alliance, placed efforts on restoring the imperial rule, and was a prominent figure in the movement to overthrow the Tokugawa Shogunate.

** Satsuma: Feudal domain of the Edo period, corresponding to the region around Kagoshima Prefecture today. Many influential figures were produced during the Bakumatsu period and the Meiji period, and formed a powerful political force alongside Chūshū in the Meiji government.

** Chōshū: Feudal domain of the Edo period, corresponding to the region around Yamaguchi Prefecture today. Many influential figures were produced during the Bakumatsu period and the Meiji period. People of Chōshū played a leading role to abolish the Tokugawa Shogunate and formed a powerful faction in the Meiji government.

not try to get benefits on the side, and that is probably one reason why Ryōma is so loved by later generations.

An ordinary person would want to get certain benefits out of a particular situation. But there are people who demonstrate a different attitude. Just take a look at Takamori Saigō and Ryōma Sakamoto. We can clearly see that virtue is born in the sorts of people who possess a character where conflicting forces have been integrated.

Suppose you have authority. You have status. You have money. You are in a position to do anything you wish, even to kill people. At such times, how do you control yourself and take action? This is important. I believe virtue is born in the answer to this question.

Even though you may have power as a leader, you are being asked whether you have the strength to control yourself. At the moment, North Korea's Kim Jong-un is being tested on this point as well. Does he have enough virtue to lead 20 million people and control the army when he is still only thirty years old? As we observe what he does, that will gradually become clear.

Keep making efforts while believing in your calling, and open up a way forward

There are people who can naturally act differently from how an ordinary person would based on human instincts or animal nature and live indifferently to such perspectives. There are also people who ignore their own interests and remain impartial. While this is very difficult to practice, these sorts of people generate virtue. You must believe this.

What is more, virtue is born in people who sense their calling. Virtue is also born in those who believe that the true source of their actions or will to act is in self-discipline. It is wrong to think that virtue is born out of such things as mere worldly reputation, status or money. You must, after all, turn yourself into a self-made man with nothing but the power of self-discipline. I believe that many people will follow someone who possesses the power of self-discipline, who continues to make efforts while believing in his or her calling, and opens up a way forward. This is what causes virtue to be born.

Assert yourself calmly and gradually without being hasty

At the start of this chapter, I asked what happens when someone who is 100% involved in a religion is not accepted in other places. To use a boxing analogy, that is a situation where you must learn not just the art of offense, but also of defense. It is a question of how much you can limit the damage you suffer and deliver punches. Thus, you need the art of both offense and defense, and you must study both.

You probably have not yet done enough study of society, so you must do that. Then, become accustomed to the outside world and gradually assert yourself. This attitude of asserting yourself calmly and expressing your ability gradually is also one form of virtue. You must not be too hasty. This is yet another thing you need to know. I hope that this chapter will be helpful in some way.

CHAPTER FOUR

The Undefeated

~ How to Live Beyond the Wins and
Losses of This World ~

Lecture given on February 21, 2013
at Happy Science General Headquarters
Tokyo, Japan

1. Why Is It Difficult for the Truth to Be Understood?

The majority opinion of the people of this world is not necessarily right

This chapter has a slightly unusual title. I want to speak about the subject "The Undefeated."

I have been involved in religion for many years now, and I often feel that religious values and ways of thinking are quite different from those of the world. I often study the lives of people from the past in the same line of work as me, or more specifically, the histories of religious leaders and philosophers. Their names are still known today. I have wondered many times why these people were poorly understood in their own day and why they died without having gained recognition.

This is an era in which democracy is commonly perceived as a well-rounded political system. While I do not reject democracy altogether, some people think that it is the ultimate form of government, unable to be surpassed. However, I feel that the majority opinion of the people of this world and the consensus opinion are not necessarily right. This is how I feel as I look at history and this present era as an explorer of the Truth and a person who brings down divine revelations from the heavenly world.

Two cases when the Truth is not understood

There are two cases when the Truth is not understood. One is when the world's usual or most popular ways of thinking are the opposite of the Truth. There are cases when the Truth is not accepted by society because the majority opinion at the time is the exact opposite of philosophical or religious Truths. Simply put, the Truth is rejected from the perspective of the common knowledge of the world, or the common sense of the times.

The other case is a person who, like a visionary, is too far ahead of his or her time. If someone is too far ahead of their time, contemporaries may not understand that person and are likely to misinterpret him.

The latter applies not only to religious leaders, but to physicists and astronomers in the scientific field as well. For example, there was a scientist who said for the first time that it is not the Sun that moves around the Earth, but the Earth that moves around the Sun. In those times, people who could not understand this pressured the scientist to abandon his theory and even threatened to execute him.

There was also the man who set out by sea to prove that the world is round, but he did not find it easy to gain support. To people today, the fact that the world is round is commonly accepted and everyone knows this, but back then many people believed that the world was flat. Although nobody had been to the ends of the earth, they assumed that the sea must pour over the edge like Niagara Falls, and beyond that was a mystery. That is why there was a man who attempted to travel to India from the other direction (sailing west) to prove that the world is round.

Concepts of modern physics that reverse the common ways of thinking

On the other hand, if we look at modern physics, there seem to be quite a lot of concepts from quantum physics that overlap Buddha's Truth. In other words, there are concepts that reverse our common ways of thinking.

For example, saying that "light is a particle and at the same time a wave" provides no real information. Although this statement seems to define light, it says very little. This is the same as saying, "the sea produces waves, but it is also a solid because it can form an iceberg."

However, today that statement is accepted as the Truth. Scientists cannot explain or define light unless they perceive it as both an object and a wave. It is impossible for them to explain clearly why light can be both. It is impossible while they lack a deeper understanding.

Of course, we also make use of many things that we cannot exactly explain. For example, when telegraph lines were set up for the first time in 19th century Japan, some people hung parcels on the lines expecting them to be delivered to distant locations. This may sound like a joke to us now, but in some ways it is no laughing matter.

To the people of those times, it must have been strange and unbelievable that their words could be transmitted to their families or distant relatives. So they tried hanging packages on the telegraph wires, thinking, "If words can be transmitted, can objects be sent as well?" People may have confused the telegraph system with a ropeway, but in those days such incidents did occur.

So, when it comes to the Truth, there are two rough categories: cases where the Truth is not understood based on the common thinking in the world, and cases where it is not understood because it is ahead of its time.

2. The Modern Era Puts its Faith in "Reason"

The Socratic aesthetics: adhering to principles even to death

People who live for the Truth should not expect too much to always win approval in this world in their times, in their age, or in every situation. It is important to know this. Rather, it is often the case that the more genuine the Truth, the harder for it to be understood.

Looking back now, in some ways, we still do not understand why Socrates (469–399 B.C.) stuck to his principles, even when it came to drinking poison. I do wonder why he was so obstinate.

Socrates exposed the mistakes of other intellectuals through debate, so there were probably people who, because they had lost face, were plotting to drive Socrates into a corner by inciting the people.

Socrates himself could have avoided the death penalty if he had let go of his principles. At the age of seventy, he is said to have had a young wife and small children, but he still stuck firmly to his principles. He also ignored his disciples' pleas to flee, choosing instead to drink a cup of hemlock and die. From the Socratic aesthetics, I believe we can say that he believed his teachings would have gone in vain if he had abandoned his principles in order to survive.

Ignoring what you cannot understand is unscientific and unscholarly

Perhaps modern philosophy neglects most of the Truth taught by Socrates and ignores his dialogs. Even though the man who was basically the father, founder and pioneer of philosophy was teaching the Truth, people often write it off as the words of someone who lived 2,500 years ago and read it with a grain of salt.

In fact, Socrates taught about reincarnation and the existence of the soul, as well as the existence of guardian spirits. What is more, a guardian spirit called Daimon was constantly whispering to him. Apparently, Daimon was the type of guardian spirit who clearly said what Socrates should avoid doing, and did not specify what he should do. It is evident that Socrates spoke constantly with this being.

I presume that constitutionally, Socrates himself could not talk with many different spirits in the way I do. At any rate, he was certainly the type of person who could get an answer from a spirit quickly regarding his ideas.

However, from the time of Aristotle (384–322 B.C.), these sorts of spiritual matters were no longer understood. While Plato (427–347 B.C.) had a spiritual disposition, Aristotle did not, so from around that time onwards, people started to have difficulty understanding spiritual matters. Then, later generations leaned toward the approach of accepting only what they could understand and ignoring the rest.

Such an attitude is extremely common. I think that this is certainly not a scientific attitude, nor a scholarly one, but humans have the tendency to sweep what they do not understand under the carpet and brush it away as superstition or some kind of illusion.

Descartes and Kant clearly had faith

Another example is Descartes (1596–1650). In Discourse on Method, he talked about the dualism of body and soul. If you read the entire work, you will see that he clearly advocated faith and distinctly taught the existence of the soul and the spirit world. He also clearly stated that he himself had a predisposition to revelatory dreams.

However, modern studies skip over all of these parts. In short, for the mediocre academic or researcher, it is convenient to separate this world from the other and study only this world. That is what they are doing.

Kant (1724-1804) also followed this trend. But apparently, Kant himself was very interested in spiritual matters. He was highly interested in the supernatural powers of Swedenborg (1688-1772) and gathered much information about him.

Swedenborg, for example, could see various things from a remote distance, such as a fire occurring hundreds of miles away. In fact, he had out-of-body experiences in which he would visit the spirit world. When his soul left his body, he would appear as if dead for about three days, so he kept his servants out of his room. Thus, he would go and investigate the other world, then return.

Apparently Kant was extremely interested in him. However, even though he was interested in spiritual matters, it was an unsuitable subject for his research. Therefore, he just focused on more suitable academic topics. That is what he did, and he taught an abstract and difficult philosophy.

Kant's philosophy is extremely abstract; it is not worldly or tangible. It became somewhat difficult to understand the spirit world due to the "abstract world" he created.

Moreover, Kant himself admitted that, in a way, his philosophy acted as a "guillotine" that sliced off the head of God. Nevertheless, Kant himself did have faith and was very interested in subjects such as the activities of psychics. He merely carried out his research with a kind of austere attitude, excluding spiritual matters from his subject of academic research.

Was the civilization experiment "faith in reason" a success?

Kantian philosophy was adopted by other philosophers and thinkers, and it influenced historical events such as the French Revolution. After all, Kantian philosophy ended up being a "guillotine" that cut off the head of God, so more people started to strongly believe in human rationality and established a "faith in reason."

In other words, since it is impossible for them to actually meet God and talk with Him, people came to believe more in human rationality. But this rationality was uncertain about righteousness at the individual level. Therefore, it was decided to run society based on majority agreement, which was reached after the serious and correct discussions of numerous sober people in the daytime. And so, this sort of rational society was formed.

Related to this, we can say that royal rule was originally based on theories like the divine right of kings. God tried to govern the earth through the king because God Himself does not have a physical body.

Therefore, God sent His representatives into the royal family for generations and entrusted them to rule over this world. This theory was upheld for a long time.

For this reason, most of the remaining royal families or dynasties have a tradition of myth or the belief that they are descendants of God. The same is true of Japanese Shinto. Even now, today's Imperial Family are believed to be the descendants of Amaterasu-O-Mikami (the Sun Goddess). The theory of the divine right of kings also represents this belief.

However, this idea was rejected during the French Revolution. But no better alternative was invented, so there were numerous backlashes, and France went back and forth for a while between the rule of monarchy and republicanism.

Therefore, in the modern era, many experiments of civilization were conducted as they did not fully believe the Truth they had come across.

Those experiments also had good points. When God, Buddha or the heavenly world gives teachings, they take into account the nature of the era. But as the times change, old teachings can cause an era to stagnate and may obstruct progress. This is because the teachings that are appropriate for each and every era are not always revealed.

When people from the past have authority, it can be very hard to accept the new. That is why they started to think that they ought to create a system where they could live happily through group discussions, rather than relying on old beliefs.

In this sense, it is true to say that in the "Age of Enlightenment," or in the trends of modern enlightened philosophy and democracy, some aspects were compatible with faith. However, just like the system recognizing the emperor as the symbol of the state in Japan, there was also a trend of treating God merely as a symbol and returning what is tangible or worldly into the hands of humankind. The only realistic way to compensate for this negative aspect would be for people to try and raise the level and quality of education and faith in this world.

3. Shakyamuni Buddha's Renunciation and the Destruction of His Homeland

A Buddhist scholar gives in to post-war democracy

I have cited the example of Socrates, and the same can be said about Shakyamuni Buddha as well.

Shakyamuni Buddha was a prince of the Shakya clan and the king's only son. A Japanese Buddhist scholar Hajime Nakamura,* however, downplayed the Buddha and went along with the trend of post-war democracy. He stated that the king of the Shakya clan was not what we would call the monarch of a kingdom, but more like the chairman of an autonomous community.

This represents an example of a Buddhist scholar giving in to post-war democracy. It is impossible that someone like a democratically elected chairman would have been able to rule a country in those ancient times. Nakamura probably said that because he was embarrassed to use the word "king."

Moreover, Hajime Nakamura used the words "a human Buddha" a lot and stressed Buddha's human aspects. This is due to the trend in academic research where it is considered shameful to believe in anything mythical.

---

* Hajime Nakamura (1912 - 1999): Professor Emeritus of the University of Tokyo. He published many monographs and essays as a global authority on Indian phi-losophy, Buddhism and studies on comparative philosophy.

What if tabloids existed in Shakyamuni Buddha's day?

If we apply the current common sense to Shakyamuni Buddha's life, there are several points in which he would have been criticized if tabloids existed back then: Buddha's renunciation, his enlightenment and the history of his missionary work. It would be very easy for me to write a criticism on Buddha if I were the editor of the Japanese weekly magazine, Shincho or Bunshun:

"His parents and those around him had great expectations for him. He grew to adulthood having received an education from good tutors and learned martial skills with enthusiasm. Still, he abandoned his responsibilities as heir, sneaked out of the castle and ran away.

"His parents had done everything that they could to prevent such an unlikely event from occurring. They had even assembled the most beautiful women in the land to serve him and built him a palace for each of the three seasons (summer, monsoon and winter). He had been brought up in such luxury that he only wore clothes of the finest silk. But he threw it all away and sneaked out of the castle at dawn, renouncing the world.

"He was completely irresponsible. What was he thinking, running away after all that his parents had done for him? Although it probably turned out well for him, what about the people he left behind?"

In the end, the Shakya clan did not survive any longer than Buddha. The clan perished during the course of his life. "Shakya" is the name of the clan, and it is also used as a synonym for the country. If I were to explain this using myself as an example, I would be called Ryuho Tokushima because I was born in Tokushima Prefecture.

Although Buddha's Sangha remained, the Shakya kingdom came to a tragic end

In the latter years of Buddha's life, the Shakya clan was destroyed by a larger country called Kosala. In those days, India consisted of sixteen countries, and the two most powerful nations, Magadha and Kosala, were continually vying for supremacy. After having renounced the world, Buddha had a base called Jetavana Monastery in Kosala, and one called Venuvana Monastery in Magadha. Thus, he had bases in both of the powerful states. This signifies that Buddha was politically neutral, or rather that he transcended politics.

Magadha and Kosala formed marriage alliances, but were forever going to war with one another. The Shakya kingdom was a kind of a vassal state of Kosala. Although Buddha created his Sangha there, the country itself perished during Buddha's latter life. Prior to that, Buddha had drawn around 500 people into his Sangha, including young people and some of his relatives. However, not everyone renounced the world, so when the kingdom perished, the others met an extremely tragic end.

Buddha's teachings themselves had spread to his homeland. In those teachings was also a way of thinking that is rather similar to ahimsa (no destruction of life), so the Shakya kingdom only defended itself and did not put up any resistance, resulting in the near-complete annihilation of the entire clan. In that respect, it bears a slight resemblance to Japan today.

When I find those who bear the name "Shakya" among Nepalese Happy Science believers, I marvel at the fact that there were survivors and I wonder where they fled. The Shakya clan was nearly annihilated and there should have been no survivors. One group probably hid and escaped, then stayed in hiding, so that today there are still people with the name "Shakya."

In his final years, Buddha witnessed the fall of his homeland. He set out on a final journey toward his defeated homeland before entering Nirvana. This world can be pitiless indeed.

In any case, Buddha renounced his duty of protecting his country as heir of the royal household, deserted his wife and son, and abandoned everything to enter the path he sought. He did create a Sangha, so he can be said to have achieved a certain degree of success as an individual. But in those days, his group was only one of a number of influential religious organizations in India. His teachings did not spread as far as throughout the whole of India. They spread from Central India, around the middle reaches of the Ganges. However, it has been said that there were other influential religious leaders.

So, there are many points where the Buddha is vulnerable to criticism. Nevertheless, Buddhist believers do not say anything about these.

There are myths and legends in rational Buddhism as well

There are many myths and legends about the Buddha's birth. It is said that as he walked seven steps in each of the four directions, a lotus bloomed, and after that he said, "In Heaven and Earth, I alone am to be revered." It is, of course, rather difficult to walk immediately after being born, but Buddhists say nothing about that. Even though Buddhism is said to be a rational religion, they keep quiet about these sorts of mythical aspects. This is a peculiar, or rather good, characteristic of Buddhists.

Also, it is said that when the Buddha was conceived, he entered his mother's womb from the Tushita heaven in the form of a white elephant. I, too, have actually seen a soul of a different form enter a body. Many such mysterious incidents occur.

Did Jesus and the Buddha save their homeland?

The same could be said about Jesus Christ. About forty years after he was put to death, his country perished. Some people may say, "Even though Jesus was the Savior, he didn't save Judea. He was born as the Savior, but in the end, his country was destroyed."

Moreover, for 1,900 years after that, the Jews were nomad tribes, scattered around the world. Just when they had finally built a nation in the 20th century, their country became a seed of conflict in the Arab world. Thus, some people may think that Jesus was a "good-for-nothing Savior."

Similarly, even though the Buddha is also said to be the Savior, the Shakya kingdom was destroyed. So he could be criticized for not saving his homeland.

There was also an incident that is the origin of the Japanese saying, "Even the patience of a saint has limits." When King Vidudabha of Kosala came to destroy the Shakya kingdom, he saw the Buddha sitting beneath a withered tree. Upon seeing him, the king remembered that the Buddha was the prince of the Shakya clan and so withdrew his army. Some people say that it was a miracle that the Buddha appeared, but it happened three times. However, the king came to attack again, and it is said that the Buddha resigned himself to the destruction, thinking that it might be karma from a past life.

Buddhist pacifism has aspects that can invite massacres

This story remained as the saying, "Even the patience of a saint has limits." After all, this world has its own rules and King Vidudabha did have his reasons for attacking.

In fact, King Vidudabha had gone to the Shakya kingdom to study when he was a prince. But he had been terribly humiliated. It was when he first found out the truth about his mother's birth. Actually, when Kosala ordered the Shakya kingdom to send a bride from the royal family, they felt a little disgraced about doing exactly as told. So they deceitfully sent the daughter of a servant woman from the slave class. Despite having some connection with the royals, his mother was from a servant class. Vidudabha discovered this when he went to study there.

Since India was a country with a rigid caste system, the bloodline was very important. Prince Vidudabha, greatly ridiculed and humiliated by the Shakya clan, returned home furious. He vowed to take revenge on them once he became king.

Therefore, King Vidudabha had gone to take revenge. The Buddha stopped him three times, but finally came to think that the people of the Shakya clan bore a moral responsibility for this and did not stop Vidudabha any further.

When the Shakya kingdom was destroyed, many tragic incidents occurred, and these are also described in Buddhist scripture. For example, the king at that time— I think it was the Buddha's cousin— pleaded with King Vidudabha, "Please, will you give the women and children a little time to escape? Please let them go while I dive into the pond and hold my breath."

Vidudabha said, "Very well. Only for that long," but the king stayed underwater and did not resurface, no matter how long they waited. Finding it strange, Vidudabha's men dived into the water to find that the king had drowned by tying his hair to the roots of the reeds to stop his body from floating up. This tragic tale remains till today. So there was a man who even sacrificed his own life to buy time for women and children to escape. In this way, the Shakya kingdom came to a tragic end.

If turned in a negative direction, Buddhist pacifism can invite enemies to inflict terrible cruelties and commit massacres. This is one aspect of Buddhist pacifism, and a little caution is required on this point.

4. Why Unreasonable Incidents Happen in This World

The power to maintain the status quo ignores Happy Science

Various Truths are taught in all kinds of forms, yet they can all have their own vulnerabilities. It is difficult to send the perfect Truth down to this world, in a form that is flawless with no weaknesses. In reality, it can be said that the Truth often does not accord with the common thinking of this world in most cases.

I have been working for more than thirty years ever since I attained the Great Enlightenment. We have been active as a religious organization for a considerable number of years. However, my wish is far from being realized.

Happy Science expresses opinions about the direction Japan should be heading in, and we also go beyond that to express many opinions about other countries. We express our opinions about Japan's potential enemies, and even about countries that are allied with Japan. When it comes to countries ruled by other religions, we also identify the problems with those religions.

Although such matters may be somewhat beyond our current actual power, I give these opinions because it will be too late if I do not speak out now. Still, our organization is not strong enough to keep up with what I wish to accomplish.

The worldly powers that do not want to recognize Happy Science wish to maintain the status quo. They may not necessarily be malicious, but due to their past success, they have a strong tendency to stick with the old ways of thinking. That is why when a completely new way of thinking emerges and they are told to follow it, they cannot follow it right away. This power to resist is expressed in their attitude of ignoring us or refusing to comment.

A final assessment takes time

When people receive awards from the state, it generally means that their professional life is over. Put in another way, a final assessment of their contribution has practically been made and they will not rise any higher or produce anything further. Or, in many cases, people finally gain recognition after they die. There are also many instances where someone is rated extremely highly while alive. But this evaluation is overturned completely after he dies.

After all, if people are unable to see into the future, it may cause various difficulties. For example, Japan was strongly criticized for "all of the atrocities it inflicted on the neighboring countries of Asia." The post-war period began on the basis of reflecting on the lessons Japan had learned. However, if the countries that claim to have been invaded by Japan are praised too highly and treated as being completely right, that can cause another problem where the mistakes of those countries cannot be corrected.

Another example involves Mao Zedong. When he died in 1976, I remember that the Japanese newspapers of the day ran huge headlines saying, "The Death of a Great Man," and very many articles were written, extolling his greatness. But even though leaders are said to be great heroes while they are alive, various problems can sometimes surface a few years later. The same is true of Kim Il-sung and Stalin. They wielded tremendous power while they were alive, but after their death, their reputation plummeted.

Hitler is another example. He was initially a hero born from the ballot box, the democratic voting system. When he came on the scene, he was endorsed by around 90% of voters. However, even in his lifetime, he was spoken of as an evil tyrant.

Human beings can be easily blinded by the food in front of them or immediate gain and have a tendency to think, "Better to bend than to break." So when they are pressured by powerful authorities or someone who has military backing, they generally follow orders. As a result, before they know it, they may end up encountering the same kind of fate as the Jews massacred in the gas chambers.

The absurdity of this world: the case of Daw Aung San Suu Kyi

In this world, unreasonable events often happen and continue for a period of time. The Soviet Union lasted for more than seventy years. Although China still exists, I believe that I will watch it come to an end in my lifetime. God sometimes allows absurdities to go on for some decades.

The same goes for Myanmar. Countries such as England still call it "Burma," but in any case, in Myanmar, the party led by Daw Aung San Suu Kyi won a great victory in the elections of 1990. However, although she should have been mandated to lead the government, she was held under house arrest for twenty years by the military government.

Her British husband lobbied for her with all of his might so she was able to win the Nobel Peace Prize. Nevertheless, even though he tried hard to help her by focusing the attention of the world upon her, he could not get her released.

If she had accepted deportation and left Myanmar, she would never have been allowed back in. She could not leave the country. As a result, she spent twenty years under house arrest, far from her husband and children. This episode took place openly with the entire international community watching.

Although it is said that Myanmar is moving forward with democratization, in reality, there is still a military government at this point in time. They have softened a little and become able to receive some aid from foreign countries. What is happening is that some military personnel pretend to be civilians to show that they are involved in politics, when the military are in fact running the nation.

Moreover, Myanmar's Constitution has been revised so that Suu Kyi cannot become president. It is extremely difficult to revise the Constitution in Japan, but in Myanmar, the Constitution has been revised so that anyone who has had a foreign spouse cannot become president. To all intents and purposes, this is aimed at Suu Kyi. It would be understandable if they forbade someone who currently has a foreign spouse. That is because a foreign country could control the nation through the spouse. But this does not apply to Suu Kyi's situation because her husband has already passed away.

When Myanmar's Constitution was revised, two articles were inserted: "Anyone who has had a foreign spouse cannot become president," and, "Anyone who has no knowledge of military affairs cannot become president." In other words, you cannot become president unless you have been a soldier or a member of the military.

As a result of these two articles, Suu Kyi virtually cannot become president. It is surprising that articles have to be inserted into a constitution to prevent a particular person from becoming head of state. I would quite like these people to come to Japan and revise our Constitution. But in any case, there is a country where such things can be done.

Having said this, however, the democratic movement in Myanmar is still active today, so this Constitution will probably be scrapped in time. As you can see, these kinds of unreasonable events are fairly common, and can last twenty years or more.

The Pol Pot era, when there were living devils

There are also cases such as the former Pol Pot regime of Cambodia, which killed two million of its citizens and turned them into skeletons. This was genocide; huge numbers of skulls laid on shelves, forming mountains of human skulls. It was mostly intellectuals and the intelligentsia who were killed. Everyone who had graduated from university was killed, including students who had returned to Cambodia after studying or living abroad.

These people were killed because they acquired different values. It is usually the educated intellectuals who criticize what the statesmen are doing. People who know how governments work overseas will criticize politicians, so all of the intellectuals and those who had been abroad were killed. This is unacceptable. If it were Happy Science, it would be the staff in our International Headquarters who would all be killed off first. That is because they could find plenty to criticize by drawing on examples from other countries.

So, in the face of an atrocity in which two million citizens of a country are killed, in reality, it can be the case that nothing can be done. There are times like this when living devils exist.

Righteousness verified by history becomes wisdom for humankind

This world is a kind of an experimental site, a place to learn various lessons. From that point of view, cruel or unreasonable events may occur for a certain period of time. However, people begin to reflect upon them once it is over and contemplate on "what is right" until it becomes wisdom for humankind. Therefore, what is right sometimes cannot be understood at the time.

In 3rd century China, for example, there was a time when three kingdoms were forever fighting each other, and this is described in the Records of the Three Kingdoms. During that time, nobody knew which kingdom represented justice and most people probably merely thought that the winning kingdom should unify the land.

If we look at history, we cannot easily see a logical unfolding. Rather than having been constructed logically in a straight line, history seems to consist of both "construction" and "destruction."

5. Endure Not Being Approved Of

The ups and downs of staff in the early stages of Happy Science

Happy Science has been developing various projects and is doing various kinds of work, but I feel that we are not yet sufficiently approved of and things often do not go as we have planned. Sometimes I think, "Why do people obstruct us and try to interfere with our work when we are trying so hard?" and, with regard to other organizations, I sometimes wonder, "Why do people praise such bad organizations so fervently?"

It is probably because the people or groups who are mistaken often have a closer affinity with this world, and their values are closer to those of this world. So they can be easily understood and seem familiar. Therefore, people who live for the Truth must endure not being approved of for a certain period of time. It is necessary to have this mindset.

I used to look back at the past and think a lot, "My work doesn't proceed as I have planned," or, "We are doing such good things, but why can't people understand it?" However, when I recall my past and think back to before Happy Science was founded, or before I started communicating with the Real World, I had no disciples. I, myself, did not know the Truth.

Then I experienced spiritual phenomena and at first, even my family regarded them doubtfully and thought it unbelievable. So my work began when my family started to believe.

After that, when I started coming out with books, many people became my readers and the avid ones gradually gathered to support me. Since then, decades have passed. There have been many changes, with various ups and downs.

Initially my family helped me but later, disciples of other organizations joined us and helped out in various ways. However, as our organization became established, those relationships became difficult.

Disciples who came from other organizations tended to think that the earlier they joined, the greater they were. If someone greater emerges from among disciples who joined later, it makes the relationship with the earlier ones extremely difficult. I do not always promote people in the order in which they joined us. When I select people to promote, it is difficult to always take this factor into consideration. So sometimes I felt sorry for some of the managers who were with us at the start.

Some people might have stayed longer if they had joined us a little later. However, in many cases, they decided to leave earlier than expected since they arrived too soon before the organization firmed up. Some people, who were accustomed to the free and flexible atmosphere of Happy Science in the earlier stages, found that they gradually lost their freedom as the management became more structured. They could no longer act or give directions as they pleased. As a result, many changes occurred around me.

An attitude of patiently adhering to the Truth is important

Among people who are not members of Happy Science, there have been supporters and opponents, as well as those who had a change of heart and reversed their opinion of us. Through these decades, we experienced various battles.

Besides Happy Science, there are also other religions that were founded in Japan in the 1980s. Although people considered us all to be similar in the beginning, I feel that their assessment gradually changed as the years passed.

People used to attack us, believing in their hearts that Happy Science was a mistaken religion. But the reason for their attacks gradually changed. Given that Happy Science has a certain degree of influence and authority in society, people have started to keep an eye on the movement of influential religions, just as influential politicians are kept under surveillance. I get the feeling that the nature of their attack is therefore changing.

Nevertheless, from our point of view, we are still far from realizing the Truth. So we cannot stop here. If we ceaselessly aim to move one step higher, we may seem to be lusting for power and fame, and could be criticized even more intensely. So we will continue to face hardships that we feel we can barely overcome.

We are waging the "war of Truth" by advocating "righteousness" with all our might. However, with regard to the question, "What is righteousness?" there is a big difference between the righteousness that is valid even in the spirit world and a righteousness that is valid only in this world. These two do not easily coincide.

Despite that, I feel that society is gradually recognizing what Happy Science is saying and following us within a comparatively short period of time, though it may be little by little. But as our basic stance, I often remind myself that we must be patient.

Although we must keep growing, we also need to know that it is difficult to achieve rapid success or a huge expansion. Unlike in the world of entertainment or sports, a religion can rarely become a superstar overnight. Rather, there are even times when we find it unreasonable to see other religious organizations in the limelight, receiving attention or being praised highly.

However, while we persevere patiently, those who were praised to the skies may suddenly find their reputations plummeting. I have seen this happen time and time again in the past. Therefore, even if other organizations are treated as the flavor of the month, we must not be taken in by that or go into battle hastily. Rather, the attitude to adhere firmly to what we think and believe is important.

6. Messengers of God Who Died for the Truth

Strangely enough, those who change history must undergo ordeals

At this point in time, I am not so radical as to wish to advance our activities rapidly to the extent that they trigger a disastrous future for us. However, as can be seen from the history of humankind, people who change history have all been faced with rather harsh ordeals. In some ways, I do not know how the future will be.

For example, when we look at the life of Shōin Yoshida (1830-1859), the forerunner of the Meiji Restoration in Japan, I cannot help but wonder why he was eventually executed. If there was a reason for his execution, it was probably that he had been too strong of an influence. In other words, people in authority may have thought that since Yoshida was too influential, he would gain a great many believers and supporters, so they decided to nip him in the bud. But even so, it does seem strange that he was executed.

Another example is Joan of Arc (1412-1431) who appeared in France. That was a time when the meaning of justice had been lost. Although English and French royalty intermarried to create family alliances, England had launched a war on France. The people caught up in that upheaval probably found it hard to decide whether it would be better for France to become a colony of England, or if it was right for France to maintain its independence as a separate country.

At that time, Joan of Arc came onto the scene and made it clear that it was the Will of God to protect France. She fought a war to drive the English army out, but afterwards Joan was accused of heresy, found guilty and finally burned at the stake, not by the English, but by the Catholic clergy of France. This was irrational and it seems slightly similar to what happened to Jesus.

In the case of Jesus, too, it was not the Romans who ordered him to be executed. Although Judea was a Roman colony, it was the Jews who sought the death penalty for Jesus. As there was some distance between the Romans and Jesus, those Romans ruling the colony felt that it may be dangerous to execute this man, so they left the sentencing to the Jews.

The judgment of the Jews was to pardon a murderer but execute Jesus. That hatred is incredible. At that time, there were three other people sentenced to die, but there was a custom of pardoning one person during festivals, so the Governor of Judea asked, "Who shall I pardon, Jesus or Barabbas?" and the Jewish crowd answered, "Pardon Barabbas." While some people say that Barabbas was condemned for being a political activist, he is generally considered to have been a robber and a murderer.

Since the Jews shouted to pardon Barabbas and execute Jesus, in the end, Jesus was put to death. So Jesus was also killed by his "own people," which is truly inexplicable.

It is possible to bestow light to future generations even if you meet a tragic end

Joan of Arc's heroic career lasted from when she was seventeen to nineteen years old. She was born a farmer's daughter and had no schooling, so apparently she could neither read nor write. Before the judgment was given, she was tricked into signing a document by being told that she would not be burned if she only signed it, but in fact it was a document that declared her testimony as a lie. This document declared that the testimony she gave about hearing the voice of God was a lie. Because she was illiterate, Joan was thus tricked. Later, she withdrew that statement but was burned at the stake.

It truly is a mystery why messengers of God are usually not accepted as they should be by the world, and suffer a tragic fate.

Joan of Arc was finally declared a saint by the Catholic Church 500 years after her death. It means the Catholic Church, out of pride, persisted in refusing to admit that they were wrong for about 500 years. The general populace would admit that they had been wrong much earlier, but the Catholic Church did not do so for 500 years.

There are similarities to the case of Shōin Yoshida. However, even if such people who lived to fulfill a grand mission meet a tragic end in worldly terms, their lives will be assessed justly in later times. They can leave a powerful light in the hearts of many.

There are very few French people who are famous for having changed history, other than Joan of Arc and Napoleon. If we look back now, the Meiji Restoration, too, had various thinkers and revolutionaries. It is clear that it was just a handful of people who lit the spark of revolution.

Keep on saying what is right rather than giving in to contemporary values

There are things that cannot easily be understood by those who live in the same era. Sometimes there are also brilliant people among the persecutors. However outstanding they may be, if they are completely immersed in the regime of the day, they cannot break free of its logic and they end up loyally fulfilling their official duty.

I'm sure that there will be many times in the future, too, when we feel that the judgments and values of this world are not necessarily right. In our pursuit of Truth, even if the judgments, decisions, and assessments in this world take a different form from what we expect, we must never disregard what we believe in. We must have the attitude that we are being tested again.

Looking back at the history of humankind, from ancient times, there were many people who never compromised the Truth, even if their lives were at stake. Some of them are later evaluated correctly, while others remain unappreciated and are regarded as heretics. There are, of course, many people who, for example, were put to death and swept away by history without ever having their honor restored. But I believe that such people have been carrying out, in their own way, another mission in some other form.

In this era, too, there are probably many such people. But it does not mean that we must go along with contemporary values; instead, we must keep on expressing what we think is right.

7. People Who Live in the Truth Are Undefeatable

The importance of perseverance, the resolve never to let go of the Truth

"The Undefeated" that I speak of does not refer to those who never lose in a worldly sense. Since I also teach the laws of success, you may think that "undefeated" refers to those who continue to succeed in this world. This may be one aspect, but there is also the opposite side.

That is to say, when it comes to the Truth or Buddha's Dharma, it must continue to transcend the value judgments of this world, status, or any winning and losing. So you must be proud to sacrifice yourself for the values of Truth that you have chosen.

I started out with no believers and now I have gotten this far. Seen objectively, the number of believers is steadily increasing throughout Japan and the world. The march of light is definitely advancing and continuing to spread.

Having said this, however, we still have a long way to go before we truly establish the faith in El Cantare on this planet. It will take time to teach people our fundamental teaching, or the concept of El Cantare, and guide them to believe that El Cantare is the core leader of various religions and Truths of this Earth.

It is no easy matter to get everyone living on Earth in this era to believe in El Cantare. We will be accepted to some extent as one of the various different religions, but after growing to a certain size, I do not think that we will be accepted so easily.

The world today has many religions including Christianity, Buddhism, Islam, Japanese Shinto and others. In some ways, I do not know how they will react when Happy Science grows really large, to the extent that other religions feel threatened by us. It is quite unpredictable how we will be evaluated, or in what ways we will be criticized or attacked.

Nonetheless, it is important to have an attitude of endurance, a resolve never to let go of the torch of Truth, no matter what happens. Great people always experience a time of perseverance.

President Lincoln was not evaluated highly in his own era

Taking the example of Lincoln (1809-1865), he has been re-evaluated in America and regarded much more highly in recent years. But considering the number of times he lost the elections, I feel that people are not good at judging people even in a democratic country like America.

Lincoln probably lost far more elections than he won. I imagine that he was actually not that popular, despite the fact that he was good at making speeches and had a magnificent personality.

He was a tall man, and had long arms and legs, like a spider, due to a kind of physical disorder. I am not sure whether it's true or not, but it was said that his arms were so long that they reached his knees. In any case, he seems to have had some slight deformity or rather, a slightly unique physique.

What is more, his face was notorious for its rather unfortunate physiognomy. Apparently, he got a fan letter from a child telling him that he would look a little better if he grew a beard. So he started to grow a beard and became the figure we know today as Lincoln.

Even a man like Lincoln did not win many elections, even though he is said to be "America's most beloved president" today. In fact, he is also the president who caused the most deaths in the history of the United States. The 600,000 plus deaths in the Civil War is the highest count of American losses. But Americans probably believe strongly that President Lincoln unified the country, prevented it from becoming divided and created a great America.

Lincoln is one of the great men now venerated like a god in a godless America. But Americans of his day did not easily recognize that. He became president and led the Civil War, and even though it ended in victory for the North, he was assassinated at the theater. It means his value was yet to be established, even to this point in time.

The Southern people probably really hated him, since he had taken away their previous property rights. In those days, slaves were also property, and the emancipation of slaves caused tremendous damage to the Southern cotton plantation business. However, Lincoln put a higher priority on the abolition of racial discrimination.

Reverend King fought to abolish racial discrimination but was finally assassinated

Although racial discrimination in America seemed to have been abolished by Lincoln, in fact it still continued nearly a hundred years later. So, even though people say that Lincoln unified the country and brought about equality, the wall that divided whites and blacks in that country still existed. For that reason, Reverend King, Martin Luther King Jr., gave his famous speech, "I Have a Dream."

In this speech, he says, "I have a dream that one day on the red hills of Georgia, the sons of former slaves and the sons of former slave owners will be able to sit down together at the table of brotherhood." But Reverend King, too, was assassinated; he was shot while holding a meeting on a motel balcony.

In this world, things often happen that make us think, "Why do such outrageous results occur?"

People with strong beliefs are undefeatable

People who live in the Truth may not be approved of; they may suffer hostility, persecution and oppression in the world of the day. However, as long as eternal values and universality accompany their work, I believe that this will always be rewarded later.

At Happy Science, too, we are doing all that we can to the best of our abilities. We are doing so in order to change the structure of Japan and the United States and to change how the Chinese government is run. Regardless of our limited power, we do such things and also express our opinions about North and South Korea, about the Arab world and other countries.

Seen objectively, we probably require more power to accomplish such things. Our actions may still be on par with throwing stones at tanks. Still, I firmly believe that with time the Truth will certainly spread. It will not shrink, but expand. I also believe that we will surely play an effective role at the turning point in history.

Of course, we want to follow a path that can also be regarded objectively as success. Even if our success is delayed, or if the road that leads to success seems to be blocked, we must continue to show that there are people in this world who are undefeated even when they lose. I strongly desire to demonstrate to future generations that people who live with profound beliefs are undefeatable.

Sacrificing yourself for the eternally undefeatable

I teach many laws related to success, but you must always remember that failing to achieve worldly success does not mean that your pursuit was mistaken. I have to state this from the perspective of religion. In fact, many times it happens that you are not actually defeated, even when you seem to have lost in a worldly sense. Accordingly, we can continue to shine brightly for all eternity.

Certainly, a very tough and difficult battle will still go on as long as people do not approve of our activities. You may think, "If only the Truth became widespread and more people believed in it," "If only more influential people would recognize our activities and assist us," "Why can't we get approval from the international community more quickly?" or "Why are we so bogged down in people's prejudice against religion and just can't break free of it?" Such thoughts may keep flooding in.

However, people who belong to other religions are doubtlessly having similar thoughts. People who believe in other religions are probably also frustrated, thinking, "Our religion is the only true religion, so why isn't it spreading? Why are we not recognized by the world?"

Or, particularly from the perspective of Buddhism or other traditional religions, Happy Science may seem to be teaching the exact opposite of what they are trying to do. For example, ever since the nuclear power plant accident, other religions have been devoting themselves to the anti-nuclear movement. For them, the "maverick" Happy Science may seem to be stirring things up, causing obstructions, and trying to deprive people of happiness by advocating the promotion of nuclear power plants.

A great number of people may think, upon seeing countries like China or North and South Korea gaining power, that these countries deserve to be happy and Japan should collapse. They think that Japan did some terrible things in the last war. Alternatively, others who have a religious disposition to some extent, like President Obama, may worry that the Japanese government is swinging to the right. They may worry that it is adopting a system that may provoke a war. In this way, in reality there are various perspectives and our own thinking is not everything.

Yet, as people who believe in the Truth,
We must not lapse into egotism,
But devote our lives to spreading the Truth.
Whether you win or lose in this world,
Or even be vanquished,
There are those who remain Undefeated.
Some things are eternally undefeatable—
That is the Truth.
Know that the Truth shall forever be undefeatable.
You must always have the fortitude
To sacrifice yourself for the sake of the Truth.
That is my message to you in this chapter.

CHAPTER FIVE

The Reversal of Your Common Sense

~ The Power of Truth That Will
Open Up the New Era ~

Lecture given on March 24, 2013
at Head Temple Shōshinkan
Tochigi, Japan

1. The Battle Against the Common Sense of the Times

Since my Great Enlightenment, I have battled for over thirty years against the lack of understanding of the Truth

This chapter is based on a lecture I gave expressing my thoughts ahead of the Great Enlightenment Celebration (a celebration held to commemorate the day of my great awakening). It is now more than thirty years since I attained the Great Enlightenment in 1981, and when I look back I feel that I have indeed been a "warrior." I feel that particularly strongly when I reflect on the most recent years of my life.

My battle is not over yet. The Wheel of Dharma has been turned, but our path ahead is still long. The darkness of spiritual ignorance is still deep. There are still many people who are far from the Truth. Although we have started going overseas to spread my teachings, I feel that my messages are still far from reaching people around the world.

I have already given the basic foundations of my teachings. Our battle from now on will be how far and how wide we can spread these teachings. Looking at the history of humankind, there is no religious leader who

did not have to fight against the worldly common sense
of his day.

How can people be so forgetful?

Why is it so hard for them to understand such simple
Truths?

Why do they so obstinately refuse to believe

In anything that they cannot see with their own eyes,

Hear with their own ears

Or touch with their own hands?

This is truly pitiful.

Jan Hus was executed for the "sin" of translating the Bible into Czech

It makes me even sadder to know that the opponents a
religious leader must fight against are not only people
who do not believe in religion. For example, among
the spiritual messages we have published recently is
*Spiritual Messages from Jan Hus and Joan of Arc.** These
two religious leaders lived around the year 1400.

If we look back today at the history of the Czech
Republic, the birthplace of Jan Hus (ca, 1370-1415), we
can see that he is the only person who can be considered

* IRH Press Co., Ltd., available only in Japanese.

a "god." There is no one else. In the portraits of Jan Hus, we also find him alone. There are no other gods or angels painted with him. He is the only guiding spirit of light who has descended to the capital of the Czech Republic (Prague). People speak of him as if he was the god who founded the country.

However, the Vatican of the day, the headquarters of the Catholic Church, judged him to be a heretic. Hus was the master at Charles University in Prague but was persecuted for having translated the Bible, which is a record of the words and actions of Jesus. Hus was persecuted for translating it into Czech and circulating it to the people. Hus was subjected to the Inquisition, condemned to death and burned at the stake.

If this had been done by irreligious people or by people of an old indigenous religion that feared new beliefs, it might be understandable. However, Hus was deemed to be a heretic by the Catholic Church because he was the first to release the Bible in Czech, and so he was burned at the stake. After that, the people's anger could not be assuaged and it gave rise to a fierce battle known as the Hussite Wars.

The Church executed Joan of Arc, a patriotic maiden who obeyed the voice of God

What followed that might not have been a full generation later, Joan of Arc, also known as "the Maid of Orleans" came onto the scene in France. She was a young maiden born into the peaceful farming village of Domremy. When she was seventeen, Joan heard the voice of God telling her to liberate Orleans from the English invaders and to save France. Then she rose to action to liberate Orleans, which at that time was surrounded by the enemy.

She continued fighting for two years, hurling herself into the thick of the fray astride her white horse and with a sword in hand. As a result, she liberated Orleans and prevented the destruction of France. The English army withdrew completely. It was indeed a miracle.

However, incredibly enough, Joan of Arc, who saved France, was subjected to the Inquisition by the Catholic Church. After being interrogated many times, she was convicted of heresy and burned to death.

She was considered a "heretic" because the Catholic Church thought it dubious that a young girl from a farming village would be able to hear the voice of God. She could neither read nor write French. They thought that the voice of God would not be sent down to someone like her when even clergymen like themselves could not hear it. They then found various pretexts on which to criticize her. For example, they asked her if she had obeyed her mother and father, based on traditional Catholic teachings, and then accused her of heresy for disobeying her parents.

However, a girl commanded by God to liberate France would never have asked for the permission of her parents. In fact, there was no difference at all between the Catholic clergy in the time of Joan of Arc and the Jewish clergy 2,000 years ago, who believed in the Old Testament and crucified Jesus.

A history of suppressing religious reformers sent from the heavenly realm

Five hundred years later, the Catholic Church finally canonized Joan of Arc. However, it was obvious to everyone in her day that she was one of God's people. It was obvious that she was simply accomplishing a sacred task God had ordered her to undertake: to liberate France and protect its independence. Everyone knew that without her, France would have been destroyed. But it took the Church five hundred years to admit that.

Recently, a new Pope was installed at the Vatican. It is said to be the first time in six hundred years that, for various reasons, the Papacy has changed hands while the former Pope is still alive. I feel that the Catholic Church was unbelievably antiquated compared to the common thinking of today.

The Vatican has been involved in various scandals, and there are even dark rumors of its involvement in shady financial transactions with the Mafia. I presume that "politicians" or "profiteers," who are under the guise of clergymen, are rampant in the Vatican. Such people who shrewdly work their way around worldly matters have no doubt continued to oppress the true religious reformers sent from the heavenly realm.

2. The Common Sense of the Religious World Tramples on God's Heart

The church does not truly want Christ's Resurrection

When the world entered the age of scientific enlightenment, religion was swept aside and people lost faith; at the same time, believing in science based on materialism became the common sense or commonly accepted knowledge in this world. This kind of common sense must be reversed, but the title of this chapter, "The Reversal of Your Common Sense," does not refer to the reversal of this alone.

In the common sense that exists solidly in religions, too, there are already ideas that trample on God's heart. There are also many people in religions who would prioritize protecting themselves ahead of God's Will. The title also refers to overturning the common thinking that exists in the religious world.

This is exactly what Dostoyevsky, a Russian writer, described through the words of the Grand Inquisitor in his book, *The Brothers Karamazov*. The chapter titled, "The Grand Inquisitor" tells the story of Jesus being resurrected on Earth in the Middle Ages. The cardinal who appears in this story understands that the man who heals the sick and restores the dead to life is indeed the second coming of Jesus.

Despite that, the cardinal has the man arrested, put in jail and interrogated. The cardinal does not give him the death sentence, but exiles him from the town. At that time in prison, the cardinal says to him something along the lines of, "I know who you are. However, we do not need you. Why have you come back now? There was no need for you to come. We do not want the world we have built to be destroyed by your return." Thus, in this book, the cardinal ordered the man's exile, fully knowing that the man was the resurrected Christ.

The Russian Orthodox Church excommunicated Tolstoy, Jesus' brother soul

In the same era as Dostoyevsky, a literary giant named Tolstoy (1828-1910) was born in Russia. We recorded his spiritual messages in 2012, and at that time, he clearly stated that he was one of Jesus' brother souls (branch spirits).*

In his spiritual messages, Tolstoy said, "While there is light, walk in the light," just as Jesus did in the past. But in fact, Tolstoy was excommunicated by the Russian Orthodox Church in his final years. Although he was a world-famous literary giant, he was excommunicated

* See *Tolstoy: Words for Life* (tentative title), IRH Press Co., Ltd., available only in Japanese

because he was deemed "unacceptable" for a believer of the Russian Orthodox Church. Similarly, this is an age when the church started by Jesus no longer understands Jesus' will.

The common sense of the 21st century is filled with vast misunderstandings and mistaken ideas

The common sense that we must now reverse is not only the thinking which circulates in this convenient world of machines. "Convenient world" means a world where objects like cars, mobile phones and the internet are popularized. Apart from this, some ways of thinking based on religious traditions must also be overturned because they have been covered with dirt and grime, dust and mold, and no longer reflect the Truth.

As in the work of literature I mentioned earlier, even if someone equivalent to Jesus or Buddha appeared in this world now, it is possible that his or her coming would actually be considered unwanted. In many cases, churches, temples and various large religious groups would want to protect themselves and ensure their group's continuation, and so make a "necessary decision" to shun such a person.

A similar attitude can be seen in the world of politics as well. There are many corrupt people who call themselves "politicians." They only wish for the continuation of existing structures so they can protect their own vested interests and livelihoods. They employ various wiles to achieve that end. In the world of religion, too, there are many priests who nonchalantly hold memorial services for the dead, when in fact, they deny the existence of the other world and the soul. This is very unfortunate.

In the world of medical science, too, doctors deny anything that cannot be proven and reject anything that is not found in textbooks. Although medical science is regarded as the culmination of the greatest modern knowledge, most medical theories completely deny spiritual phenomena. The theories treat these phenomena as mental disorders due to a malfunctioning of the brain, the mind or the nerves.

When it comes to economics, there are still a great many people who adhere to the Marxist school of economic theory. However, in our spiritual evaluation, Marx is currently in the Abyss of Hell.*

As for the psychologist Freud, the results of our spiritual investigation clearly showed that he taught a mistaken psychology.** He taught that all mental

---

* See *Spiritual Messages from Marx and Mao Zedong* (tentative title), IRH Press Co., Ltd., available only in Japanese.

** *See Spiritual Messages from Freud*, IRH Press Co., Ltd., available only in Japanese.

illnesses in human beings are rooted in abuse or sexual desire in childhood. In other words, he believed that all mental illness had a cause to be found in this world. In fact, he adopted a position where he did not need to mention matters of the soul. This, too, in itself is a kind of repudiation of religious Truth.

In this way, many children are educated in the midst of the common sense that is filled with huge misunderstandings and mistaken ideas; they are judged on their abilities and sorted into an elite. Then they enter the adult world, thinking that they are people with great common sense, and they rise in status to influence society. However, you need to be aware that the majority of today's commonly accepted knowledge is corrupt.

There are many different teachings apart from those of Happy Science, but most have crumbled and degenerated to the point that they have lost their original form. This is the situation in the 21st century.

In reality, the light of God is not reaching the world

When I went on a missionary tour to Brazil in 2010, I visited the biggest church there known as the Sao Paulo Cathedral. But when I went in, I could not feel the presence of the spirits of Paul or Jesus, and the church was spiritually empty. I was surprised to find that neither of them was present. Apparently, both spirits are interested in other countries and regions. The situation is probably much the same in other churches as well.

I found the same situation when I went on my missionary tour to Singapore. I spoke about it bluntly in my lecture there, saying, "The day before my lecture, I tried to summon the gods of Singapore. I called them many times, but only the chief of a fishing village appeared. I am sad to say that there are no gods in this country. I know it may be rude to say this, but the light of God has not reached the prosperity of Singapore, which focuses only on moneymaking. So, although atheist China and moneymaking Singapore appear to be different on the surface, in fact, there is not a big difference between the two."*

I told this straight out to the audience. In the end, I cannot help but say that growth and prosperity which lack spiritual values are truly empty. In some way or another, I want to overturn such societies.

* August 15, 2011 English lecture, "Happiness and Prosperity"

3. The Relationship Between Scientific Inquiry and Religious Truth

Searching for unknown beings in the movie Contact

Having said this, however, to my surprise, the people in this world who recognize the existence of God in various ways are still the majority. This is so, although they have no clear idea of His form or shape. For example, the movie *Contact* based on Carl Sagan's novel was made in the U.S. in 1997. It tells the story of a scientist who is trying to verify the existence of unknown beings.

Deciphering radio signals from outer space confirms the existence of interstellar transport

In this movie, for many years, a female American astronomer continues her attempts to detect signals from outer space using a radio telescope and other equipment. She believes that if there are higher life forms like those here on Earth, they must be trying to signal their existence in some form or other. Although she is trying to capture these signals, the funds supporting her research are eventually cut off and the program is about to come to an end.

That is when a radio signal arrives from Vega, in the constellation of Lyra, twenty-six light years away from Earth. When an encryption expert deciphers that signal, it turns out to be a blueprint for a vehicle transporting people to Vega.

The decision of the inquiry panel to remove an atheist from the voyage to Vega

To choose a person to board the transporter, an inquiry panel interviews about ten selected candidates to discover their aptitudes. At that time, the top candidate is the female astronomer, but she cannot give a straight answer to the question, "Do you believe in God?" She does not say that she is an atheist, but replies that she cannot believe in something for which there is no proof.

In response to this, the panel says something like the following: Since 95% of humankind believe in some kind of God, it would be inappropriate to send someone from the remaining 5% to another planet as the representative of the people on Earth. So she no longer becomes the first choice.

The previous second choice, a slightly bad-tempered older scientist boards the transporter in her place. But a fundamentalist Christian, a kind of religious cult leader, launches a terrorist attack. The transporter is destroyed and the scientist is killed in an explosion. Later in the movie, it is revealed that a back-up transporter had been built secretly in Hokkaido, Japan, and the female astronomer finally travels to Vega.

In the end, contact with Vegans is achieved

The interstellar transporter is a spherical vehicle that simply drops through something like an electromagnetic field created by rotating a device at high speeds. As it falls, the vehicle goes through a warp and travels to Vega.

After traveling through the wormhole, the astronomer arrives at Vega and meets a Vegan. The Vegan does not reveal his true form, but appears as the astronomer's deceased father and gives the following explanation.

"We have been doing this for a very long time. There are many civilizations in the universe, but not all of them have come here. Still, over the course of hundreds of millions of years, we have met the people we have invited in a form that reproduces someone in their memory."

She returns to Earth after experiencing these exchanges with an alien.

The dilemma of the female astronomer who could not prove that she had met an alien

The astronomer insists that she went to Vega, but in reality what had happened was that the spherical transporter had simply descended. So everyone around her believes that the experiment was a failure. In the footage filmed from various angles, there is only a single instant when the transporter is not on the film, but that alone does not prove that it went to Vega.

When asked, "You say that you met a Vegan but do you have any proof of that?" the female astronomer replies, "I have no proof. There is none, so if you say it was a delusion, I have no way to refute that. But I believe that what I experienced was neither a delusion, nor a fantasy. As someone who has been involved in empirical science for a long time, and as an observer, I believe that it is a memory of actually going there, not the manifestation of a delusion or a wish I have."

The point is, up until then the scientist did not believe in God and said that she could not believe in anything that could not be proved. But after she actually experienced traveling to Vega, her position reversed and now she tries to convince those who do not believe her.

No matter how much she says, "I have nothing to prove what I experienced, but I simply cannot believe that it was a delusion," she cannot prove it. Nevertheless, her own worldview is changed through the experience.

People whose lives were changed by mystical experiences of the universe

Thus, the movie *Contact* is the story of how an atheist comes to believe that there is a Great Being that created this vast universe. In fact, many people who have returned from manned flights into space such as to the surface of the moon have become missionaries or joined different religions after returning to Earth. They had mystical experiences out in the universe. Many people had them. I think this was the background to this movie.

Even the female astronomer, who had been an atheist, could no longer say that something was "mistaken" or "unbelievable" simply because there was no proof. She could no longer say so once she experienced that reality herself.

The mystery of eighteen hours' worth of white noise recorded in less than a second

What is more, there is a twist to this story. When the transporter dropped, there was an instant of less than a second when it is not seen on the film. The astronomer had taken a video camera with her to Vega and while she talked about what she was seeing, she kept filming.

All that the video camera recorded was white noise, but the footage itself was eighteen hours long. So eighteen hours had, in fact, passed in the instant that the transporter was not on the screen, and people understood that in that time she went somewhere. That was the twist to the film.

We can assume that this movie was based on a certain amount of information about outer space provided by NASA and the like. It seems that there is a fair amount of information about Vega.*

---

* See publications such as *Breaking the Silence: Interviews with Space People*, Happy Science, *Secrets of the Galactic Federation: Protectors of Earth* (tentative title), IRH Press Co., Ltd., available only in Japanese, and *The Guardian of the Universe and the Queen of Vega* (tentative title), IRH Press Co., Ltd., available only in Japanese.

The true nature of faith is to accept the "conclusion" even when there is no proof

What Happy Science is doing may be similar. People today always seek proof. They will not admit anything that has no proof unless evidence is amassed. In other words, this is an era when people will not accept something unless it is proved inductively. This is similar to a detective working on a criminal investigation. It starts with collecting fingerprints, then into amassing different kinds of proof such as material evidence, confession and testimony.

However, there is also the deductive method, which starts from the idea that there is a definite conclusion. That is why I am now gathering and publishing information about the universe and the future, using various psychic powers.

At the present point in time, there is no accumulation of any sort of evidence for what I am saying. It is not like digging up ancient layers of rock to reveal evidence that dinosaurs were alive sixty-five million years ago. There is no proof about the future, nor can evidence be produced about the universe.

However, if you can see into the future, you can look for ways to get there and explore the steps that will take you to these conclusions. The same thing applies if you can see the outcome of what will happen when you go into outer space. Therefore, the way to find the Truth is not only through the inductive method, where you reach a conclusion by accumulating real evidence. You can also do so through the deductive method, where you accept the conclusion and then explore how to get there.

The latter approach, of first accepting the conclusion, is in fact the true attitude of religion. This is exactly what religious faith is. Unless people accept the conclusion first, they will not try to understand, nor can they truly understand. In the end, everything is futile unless you accept the existence of God.

To think that the modern era is the most advanced is the height of arrogance

There are people who say, "There is nothing beyond this world" or "In this world, nothing besides what I can see, hear or feel for myself exists." To such people who only believe in what they can see with their eyes, hear with their ears, taste with their tongue or touch with their fingers, all the activities done by people who believe in religion will be a delusive fantasy. To put it in a nasty way, it's some kind of con.

There may also be many scientists who think, "Historically speaking, the age of foolishness of believing in religion has lasted at least several thousands of years for humankind. However, science has advanced and such superstitions have retreated, and in recent years we have finally emerged into a bright and shining 'open world.'"

Unfortunately, however, that is the height of arrogance. It is arrogant to think that humans have understood all Truths in the past one or two hundred years. It is also haughty to consider that two, three or four thousand years ago humankind was inferior to the people of today in terms of ethics, emotions, philosophy or the Truth. An ancient race has been excavated with a larger cranium than modern man. Since we have not met or spoken with them, it cannot be proven that they were inferior to modern-day people.

For example, even though Cro-Magnons appear to have had a bigger brain than modern people, today we cannot reproduce their thinking, culture or civilization. These can sometimes be discovered if I conduct past-life readings with an advanced psychic power. This power corresponds to the "knowledge of previous lifetimes," which is one of the Six Divine Powers.* But at the present point in time, nothing can be produced as evidence.

* See *Secrets of the Everlasting Truths*, IRH Press Co., Ltd.

However, the mere fact that there is no evidence does not mean that something does not exist.

"Spiritual Messages - Open Session" series challenges today's common sense

In the very early days of Happy Science, for a brief time I published a great number of spiritual messages as evidence that the spirit world exists. But after that, I switched my focus to theoretical works based on my own thinking, and for a long time I have been actively compiling my teachings.

However, since about 2010 I have once again been producing many books of spiritual messages as the "Spiritual Messages - Open Session" series.*

More than 300 spirits appear in this series (as of December 2013), and by publishing so many spiritual messages, I am challenging the common sense of today. I am putting forward the question, "Do you think that these spiritual messages are genuine or fake?"

On seeing how the major newspapers continue to run advertisements for my books, I think they at least understand that Happy Science is not a group of social weirdos. At the same time, they seem to think, "Ryuho

* See *The Ryuho Okawa the Truth About Lemuria*, IRH Press Co., Ltd., available only in Japanese.

Okawa seems to be sane. He seems to come to very logical and intelligent conclusions, and to say very reasonable things."

In fact, it would probably be more difficult to prove that Happy Science is crazy. Thus, we have now established a kind of authority, and we are demonstrating the ideal form of various aspects of life and ways of thinking, as well as posing the question, "What is righteousness?"

4. The Power of Truth That Shatters Mistaken Common Sense

Messages from Heaven have started to shake the world

As I mentioned earlier, the "righteousness" that Happy Science indicates to the world is fundamentally the power, light and way of thinking. These come down from the heavens, from the center of the universe and from the heart of the heavenly realm. Of course, it also includes the conclusions reached through various spiritual experiments, since continually publishing many spiritual messages is also a form of proof that is easy to understand in a worldly sense. There should be no one other than myself who can come out with such a variety of spiritual messages.

I'm not sure whether the theory of probability should be applied to this. In fact, the probability of someone being able to publish books of spiritual messages from hundreds of people who have departed from this world might be one in a million. The probability might be one in ten million, or even one in a hundred million. Perhaps it is almost impossible to express this as a probability.

Nonetheless, I keep coming out with books of spiritual messages. These spiritual messages are now starting to shake the Christian world, the Islamic world, the world of Japanese Shinto and also various atheist

227

countries. It is therefore a fact that a huge spiritual movement is starting to happen.

These spiritual messages also include messages from the gods who created Japan. For example, the gods described in *Records of Ancient Matters* and *The Chronicles of Japan* also make their appearance. This means that they are probably thinking of re-creating this country of Japan once again and pointing to a new departure by building the country afresh. By doing so, they are trying to exert a significant influence on the world's religions.

As for Christianity, I have also confirmed that neither Jesus nor Paul is present in the Christian country of Brazil, where nearly 70% of the population are said to be Catholics. Despite that, Jesus often visits Happy Science and provides spiritual guidance. The Vatican may find this truly unacceptable. They probably think that Jesus does not speak any language other than Italian. I am sorry to say that he is kind enough to speak in Japanese as well.

However, Jesus will not speak in Japanese churches. This may seem quite unfair to Christians, who perhaps think that Jesus ought to descend to places where people believe in Him and pray to the crucifix. He might pay a visit to a company that makes Christmas cakes. At any rate, I know that he does not seem to visit churches for some reason. It is probably because he knows, as I mentioned earlier, that if he appeared in a church today, he would quickly be suppressed.

The responsibility of modern people who twist spiritual Truth into materialism

There is still a tendency in Christianity to deny mystical or spiritual things. In Buddhism, too, after the passage of 2,500 years, it is possible to extract a materialistic way of thinking from the teachings by picking out just one part.

Let us say, for example, that I gave the following teaching: "I'm sure that many of you wish to live a long time. You probably want to lead a long and happy life, to live in happiness and prosperity. However, each and every one of you will one day leave this world. However much you train your physical body, whatever health regimes you follow, you will surely die some decades from now. When you die, your body will be cremated and turned into ashes, and be placed in a grave. Recently, there have also been 'natural burials' where the ashes are scattered in the sea or the mountains, but ultimately you will become ashes."

From this teaching, if you only pick up on, "When you die, you will become ash," you could interpret it as materialism saying, "Ah, people become nothing when they die; that is the end."

In fact, there is nothing wrong with the original teaching. But there are people who see it in the light of their own personal view of life. They extract and pass on only the aspects that are convenient from their current position. I believe the responsibility for what has happened lies with these sorts of people.

Shōin Yoshida is believed to be a divine being

In the heavenly realm there are beings known as buddhas and gods, as well as many angels of light and bodhisattvas who assist them. That is how it should be.

Many angels of light and bodhisattvas descend to Earth time and again, and try to guide the people here on Earth. From this we can deduce that buddhas and gods really do exist. If such high spirits did not exist and humans were left neglected, we would be unable to sense the love and compassion of the buddhas and gods.

A while ago, I went to see Shōin Yoshida's Shōka Village School and Shōin Shrine in Hagi, Yamaguchi. It's only been about 150 years since Shōin Yoshida passed away, but the shrine that venerates him is already splendid. The Shinto archways are a double construction, erected not only at the entrance of the path leading to the shrine, but also as far as the main inner shrine. Seeing this, we can quickly tell that Shōin Yoshida is the foremost god in Yamaguchi Prefecture. It is still only just over a century since his death. But there is a clear sense that he is already being treated as someone with divinity, and that no one doubts he is a god.

However, in terms of what Shōin Yoshida accomplished while he was alive in this world, he became a samurai who had no master after leaving his hometown without the permission of his feudal clan. He visited various places in other feudal clans, such as the shores, to check on them from the perspective of Japan's national defense. He made an attempt to go to America by boarding Perry's ship at Shimoda. As a result, he was arrested and imprisoned in Noyama jail and was eventually executed at a prison house in Kodenma-chō.

From a worldly point of view, his life was a history of failures. He died at the age of twenty-nine years and two months. However, the shrine where he is venerated has now become a huge monument. This means people understand that he is essentially a divine being, regardless of the fact that he was a person who lived just over a century ago.

The Chōshū region produced many great men in the 19th century, but people clearly understand that he was in a different class. This is what I sensed at that time.

The tank of Truth crushes the delusion called "common sense"

Although Happy Science still has not spread throughout the whole of Japan and there are places overseas it has yet to reach, I do have a certain level of trust in humankind. I think that what we are doing and saying will definitely be recognized throughout the world in the near future, at least during the 21st century.

What we are saying may be considered absurd from the perspective of the "textbook-level" common sense taught in schools and the common sense of traditional religions that was handed down to the present day.

However, it is clearly written in the Buddhist scriptures that Shakyamuni Buddha possessed the Six Divine Powers. It is also written that he could clearly see the past, present and future and that he was capable of "astral travel." I actually do these same things now. Many people simply cannot understand this because they read these scriptures as mere folk tales. Yet, there is someone who can actually do such things.

We are now trying to crush the way of thinking of this world and the common sense transmitted by the mass media. We are also trying to crush the traditional common sense of religions.

The Truth is strong.
The tank of Truth
Shall surely crush delusions and push forth.
Eventually the day shall come
When the people of the world can understand

The meaning of the words I always speak—
Dying for the Truth.

Please stay strong for that day.
Please cherish your faith for years and years to come.
I sincerely wish so from the bottom of my heart.

Postscript

I have cited many examples from the four great saints - Shakyamuni Buddha, Jesus Christ, Socrates and Confucius - to Jan Hus, Joan of Arc, Lincoln and Shōin Yoshida. People who have left their mark on history did not necessarily sail smoothly through their lives.

No matter how much you suffer, the Truth will gradually shine forth as you continue to endure hardships. Therefore, simply strengthen your mind and keep making constant efforts in times of endurance, however ordinary they may be.

Eventually, you will come out of your slump and overcome your hardships. And, as you try and aim to reverse the common sense, you will one day understand that people can be "undefeated" even if they seem to have lost in this world. In that process, you may sometimes feel that virtue is being generated.

We have already gone beyond the limits of the common sense of this world. All we can do is to keep fighting with an indomitable heart.

December 2013
Master & CEO of Happy Science Group
Ryuho Okawa

ABOUT THE AUTHOR

Founder and CEO of Happy Science Group.

Ryuho Okawa was born on July 7th 1956, in Tokushima, Japan. After graduating from the University of Tokyo with a law degree, he joined a Tokyo-based trading house. While working at its New York headquarters, he studied international finance at the Graduate Center of the City University of New York. In 1981, he attained Great Enlightenment and became aware that he is El Cantare with a mission to bring salvation to all humankind.

In 1986, he established Happy Science. It now has members in over 165 countries across the world, with more than 700 branches and temples as well as 10,000 missionary houses around the world.

He has given over 3,450 lectures (of which more than 150 are in English) and published over 3,000 books (of which more than 600 are Spiritual Interview Series), and many are translated into 40 languages. Along with *The Laws of the Sun* and *The Laws Of Messiah*, many of the books have become best sellers or million sellers. To date, Happy Science has produced 25 movies. The original story and original concept were given by the Executive Producer Ryuho Okawa. He has also composed music and written lyrics of over 450 pieces.

Moreover, he is the Founder of Happy Science University and Happy Science Academy (Junior and Senior High School), Founder and President of the Happiness Realization Party, Founder and Honorary Headmaster of Happy Science Institute of Government and Management, Founder of IRH Press Co., Ltd., and the Chairperson of NEW STAR PRODUCTION Co., Ltd. and ARI Production Co., Ltd.

WHAT IS EL CANTARE?

El Cantare means "the Light of the Earth," and is the Supreme God of the Earth who has been guiding humankind since the beginning of Genesis. He is whom Jesus called Father and Muhammad called Allah, and is *Ame-no-Mioya-Gami*, Japanese Father God. Different parts of El Cantare's core consciousness have descended to Earth in the past, once as Alpha and another as Elohim. His branch spirits, such as Shakyamuni Buddha and Hermes, have descended to Earth many times and helped to flourish many civilizations. To unite various religions and to integrate various fields of study in order to build a new civilization on Earth, a part of the core consciousness has descended to Earth as Master Ryuho Okawa.

Alpha is a part of the core consciousness of El Cantare who descended to Earth around 330 million years ago. Alpha preached Earth's Truths to harmonize and unify Earth-born humans and space people who came from other planets.

Elohim is a part of El Cantare's core consciousness who descended to Earth around 150 million years ago. He gave wisdom, mainly on the differences of light and darkness, good and evil.

Ame-no-Mioya-Gami (Japanese Father God) is the Creator God and the Father God who appears in the ancient literature, *Hotsuma Tsutae*. It is believed that He descended on the foothills of Mt. Fuji about 30,000 years ago and built the Fuji dynasty, which is the root of the Japanese civilization. With justice as the central pillar, Ame-no-Mioya-Gami's teachings spread to ancient civilizations of other countries in the world.

Shakyamuni Buddha was born as a prince into the Shakya Clan in India around 2,600 years ago. When he was 29 years old, he renounced the world and sought enlightenment. He later attained Great Enlightenment and founded Buddhism.

Hermes is one of the 12 Olympian gods in Greek mythology, but the spiritual Truth is that he taught the teachings of love and progress around 4,300 years ago that became the origin of the current Western civilization. He is a hero that truly existed.

Ophealis was born in Greece around 6,500 years ago and was the leader who took an expedition to as far as Egypt. He is the God of miracles, prosperity, and arts, and is known as Osiris in the Egyptian mythology.

Rient Arl Croud was born as a king of the ancient Incan Empire around 7,000 years ago and taught about the mysteries of the mind. In the heavenly world, he is responsible for the interactions that take place between various planets.

Thoth was an almighty leader who built the golden age of the Atlantic civilization around 12,000 years ago. In the Egyptian mythology, he is known as god Thoth.

Ra Mu was a leader who built the golden age of the civilization of Mu around 17,000 years ago. As a religious leader and a politician, he ruled by uniting religion and politics.

ABOUT HAPPY SCIENCE

Happy Science is a global movement that empowers individuals to find purpose and spiritual happiness and to share that happiness with their families, societies, and the world. With more than 12 million members around the world, Happy Science aims to increase awareness of spiritual truths and expand our capacity for love, compassion, and joy so that together we can create the kind of world we all wish to live in.

Activities at Happy Science are based on the Principle of Happiness (Love, Wisdom, Self-Reflection, and Progress). This principle embraces worldwide philosophies and beliefs, transcending boundaries of culture and religions.

Love teaches us to give ourselves freely without expecting anything in return; it encompasses giving, nurturing, and forgiving.

Wisdom leads us to the insights of spiritual truths, and opens us to the true meaning of life and the will of God (the universe, the highest power, Buddha).

Self-Reflection brings a mindful, nonjudgmental lens to our thoughts and actions to help us find our truest selves—the essence of our souls—and deepen our connection to the highest power. It helps us attain a clean and peaceful mind and leads us to the right life path.

Progress emphasizes the positive, dynamic aspects of our spiritual growth–actions we can take to manifest and spread happiness around the world. It's a path that not only expands our soul growth, but also furthers the collective potential of the world we live in.

PROGRAMS AND EVENTS

The doors of Happy Science are open to all. We offer a variety of programs and events, including self-exploration and self-growth programs, spiritual seminars, meditation and contemplation sessions, study groups, and book events.

Our programs are designed to:
* Deepen your understanding of your purpose and meaning in life
* Improve your relationships and increase your capacity to love unconditionally
* Attain peace of mind, decrease anxiety and stress, and feel positive
* Gain deeper insights and a broader perspective on the world
* Learn how to overcome life's challenges
   ... and much more.

For more information, visit <u>happy-science.org</u>.

CONTACT INFORMATION

Happy Science is a worldwide organization with branches and temples around the globe. For a comprehensive list, visit the worldwide directory at *happy-science.org*. The following are some of the many Happy Science locations:

UNITED STATES AND CANADA

New York
79 Franklin St., New York, NY 10013, USA
Phone: 1-212-343-7972
Fax: 1-212-343-7973
Email: ny@happy-science.org
Website: happyscience-usa.org

New Jersey
66 Hudson St., #2R, Hoboken, NJ 07030, USA
Phone: 1-201-313-0127
Email: nj@happy-science.org
Website: happyscience-usa.org

Chicago
2300 Barrington Rd., Suite #400,
Hoffman Estates, IL 60169, USA
Phone: 1-630-937-3077
Email: chicago@happy-science.org
Website: happyscience-usa.org

Florida
5208 8th St., Zephyrhills, FL 33542, USA
Phone: 1-813-715-0000
Fax: 1-813-715-0010
Email: florida@happy-science.org
Website: happyscience-usa.org

Atlanta
1874 Piedmont Ave., NE Suite 360-C
Atlanta, GA 30324, USA
Phone: 1-404-892-7770
Email: atlanta@happy-science.org
Website: happyscience-usa.org

San Francisco
525 Clinton St.
Redwood City, CA 94062, USA
Phone & Fax: 1-650-363-2777
Email: sf@happy-science.org
Website: happyscience-usa.org

Los Angeles
1590 E. Del Mar Blvd., Pasadena, CA
91106, USA
Phone: 1-626-395-7775
Fax: 1-626-395-7776
Email: la@happy-science.org
Website: happyscience-usa.org

Orange County
16541 Gothard St. Suite 104
Huntington Beach, CA 92647
Phone: 1-714-659-1501
Email: oc@happy-science.org
Website: happyscience-usa.org

San Diego
7841 Balboa Ave. Suite #202
San Diego, CA 92111, USA
Phone: 1-626-395-7775
Fax: 1-626-395-7776
E-mail: sandiego@happy-science.org
Website: happyscience-usa.org

Hawaii
Phone: 1-808-591-9772
Fax: 1-808-591-9776
Email: hi@happy-science.org
Website: happyscience-usa.org

Kauai
3343 Kanakolu Street, Suite 5
Lihue, HI 96766, USA
Phone: 1-808-822-7007
Fax: 1-808-822-6007
Email: kauai-hi@happy-science.org
Website: happyscience-usa.org

Toronto

845 The Queensway
Etobicoke, ON M8Z 1N6, Canada
Phone: 1-416-901-3747
Email: toronto@happy-science.org
Website: happy-science.ca

Vancouver

#201-2607 East 49th Avenue,
Vancouver, BC, V5S 1J9, Canada
Phone: 1-604-437-7735
Fax: 1-604-437-7764
Email: vancouver@happy-science.org
Website: happy-science.ca

INTERNATIONAL

Tokyo

1-6-7 Togoshi, Shinagawa,
Tokyo, 142-0041, Japan
Phone: 81-3-6384-5770
Fax: 81-3-6384-5776
Email: tokyo@happy-science.org
Website: happy-science.org

Seoul

74, Sadang-ro 27-gil,
Dongjak-gu, Seoul, Korea
Phone: 82-2-3478-8777
Fax: 82-2-3478-9777
Email: korea@happy-science.org
Website: happyscience-korea.org

London

3 Margaret St.
London, W1W 8RE United Kingdom
Phone: 44-20-7323-9255
Fax: 44-20-7323-9344
Email: eu@happy-science.org
Website: www.happyscience-uk.org

Taipei

No. 89, Lane 155, Dunhua N. Road,
Songshan District, Taipei City 105, Taiwan
Phone: 886-2-2719-9377
Fax: 886-2-2719-5570
Email: taiwan@happy-science.org
Website: happyscience-tw.org

Sydney

516 Pacific Highway, Lane Cove North,
2066 NSW, Australia
Phone: 61-2-9411-2877
Fax: 61-2-9411-2822
Email: sydney@happy-science.org

Kuala Lumpur

No 22A, Block 2, Jalil Link Jalan Jalil
Jaya 2, Bukit Jalil 57000,
Kuala Lumpur, Malaysia
Phone: 60-3-8998-7877
Fax: 60-3-8998-7977
Email: malaysia@happy-science.org
Website: happyscience.org.my

Sao Paulo

Rua. Domingos de Morais 1154,
Vila Mariana, Sao Paulo SP
CEP 04010-100, Brazil
Phone: 55-11-5088-3800
Email: sp@happy-science.org
Website: happyscience.com.br

Kathmandu

Kathmandu Metropolitan City,
Ward No. 15, Ring Road, Kimdol,
Sitapaila Kathmandu, Nepal
Phone: 977-1-427-2931
Email: nepal@happy-science.org

Jundiai

Rua Congo, 447, Jd. Bonfiglioli
Jundiai-CEP, 13207-340, Brazil
Phone: 55-11-4587-5952
Email: jundiai@happy-science.org

Kampala

Plot 877 Rubaga Road, Kampala
P.O. Box 34130 Kampala, UGANDA
Phone: 256-79-4682-121
Email: uganda@happy-science.org

ABOUT HS PRESS

HS Press is an imprint of IRH Press Co., Ltd. IRH Press Co., Ltd., based in Tokyo, was founded in 1987 as a publishing division of Happy Science. IRH Press publishes religious and spiritual books, journals, magazines and also operates broadcast and film production enterprises. For more information, visit *okawabooks.com*.

Follow us on:

f Facebook: Okawa Books

▶ Youtube: Okawa Books

𝒫 Pinterest: Okawa Books

◎ Instagram: OkawaBooks

🐦 Twitter: Okawa Books

g Goodreads: Ryuho Okawa

——— **NEWSLETTER** ———

To receive book related news, promotions and events, please subscribe to our newsletter below.

⌇ eepurl.com/bsMeJj

——— **AUDIO / VISUAL MEDIA** ———

YOUTUBE

PODCAST

Introduction of Ryuho Okawa's titles; topics ranging from self-help, current affairs, spirituality, religion, and the universe.

BOOKS BY RYUHO OKAWA

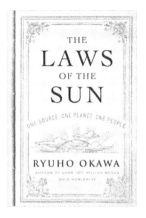

THE LAWS OF THE SUN
ONE SOURCE, ONE PLANET, ONE PEOPLE

ISBN: 978-1-942125-43-3
$15.95

IMAGINE IF YOU COULD ASK GOD why He created this world and what spiritual laws He used to shape us—and everything around us. If we could understand His designs and intentions, we could discover what our goals in life should be and whether our actions move us closer to those goals or farther away.

At a young age, a spiritual calling prompted Ryuho Okawa to outline what he innately understood to be universal truths for all humankind. In *The Laws of the Sun*, Okawa outlines these laws of the universe and provides a road map for living one's life with greater purpose and meaning.

In this powerful book, Ryuho Okawa reveals the transcendent nature of consciousness and the secrets of our multidimensional universe and our place in it. By understanding the different stages of love and following the Buddhist Eightfold Path, he believes we can speed up our eternal process of development. *The Laws of the Sun* shows the way to realize true happiness—a happiness that continues from this world through the other.

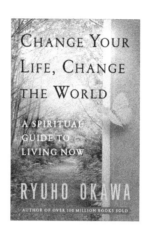

CHANGE YOUR LIFE, CHANGE THE WORLD
A SPIRITUAL GUIDE TO LIVING NOW

ISBN: 978-0-9826985-0-1
$16.95 (Paperback)

MASTER RYUHO OKAWA calls out to people of all nations to remember their true spiritual roots and to build our planet into a united Earth of peace, prosperity, and happiness. With the spiritual wisdom contained in this book, each and every one of us can change our lives and change the world.

"To save the seven billion people on Earth, God has countless angels working constantly, every day, on His behalf." — Chapter 3

THE MOMENT OF TRUTH
BECOME A LIVING ANGEL TODAY

ISBN: 978-0-9826985-7-0
$14.95 (Paperback)

MASTER OKAWA shows that we are essentially spiritual beings and that our true and lasting happiness is not found within the material world but rather in acts of unconditional and selfless love toward the greater world. These pages reveal God's mind, His mercy, and His hope that many of us will become living angels that shine light onto this world.

THE NINE DIMENSIONS
UNVEILING THE LAWS OF ETERNITY

ISBN: 978-0-9826985-6-3
$15.95 (Paperback)

THIS BOOK IS YOUR GATE TO HEAVEN. In this book, Master Okawa shows that God designed this world and the vast, wondrous world of our afterlife as a school with many levels through which our souls learn and grow. This book is a window into the mind of our loving God, who encourages us to grow into greater angels.

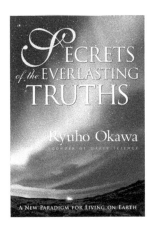

SECRETS OF
THE EVERLASTING TRUTHS
A NEW PARADIGM FOR LIVING ON EARTH

ISBN: 978-1-937673-10-9
$14.95 (Paperback)

OUR BELIEF IN THE INVISIBLE IS OUR FUTURE. It is our knowledge about the everlasting spiritual laws and our belief in the invisible that will make it possible for us to solve the world's problems and bring our entire planet together. When you discover the secrets in this book, your view of yourself and the world will be changed dramatically and forever.

ALSO BY RYUHO OKAWA

THE TEN PRINCIPLES FROM EL CANTARE VOLUME I
Ryuho Okawa's First Lectures on His Basic Teachings

THE TEN PRINCIPLES FROM EL CANTARE VOLUME II
Ryuho Okawa's First Lectures on His Wish to Save the World

THE GOLDEN LAWS
History through the Eyes of the Eternal Buddha

THE STARTING POINT OF HAPPINESS
A Practical and Intuitive Guide to Discovering Love, Wisdom, and Faith

LOVE, NURTURE, AND FORGIVE
A Handbook to Add a New Richness to Your Life

AN UNSHAKABLE MIND
How to Overcome Life's Difficulties

THE ORIGIN OF LOVE
On the Beauty of Compassion

INVINCIBLE THINKING
An Essential Guide for a Lifetime of Growth, Success, and Triumph

GUIDEPOSTS TO HAPPINESS
Prescriptions for a Wonderful Life

THE LAWS OF HAPPINESS
Love, Wisdom, Self-Reflection and Progress

TIPS TO FIND HAPPINESS
Creating a Harmonious Home
for Your Spouse, Your Children, and Yourself

THE PHILOSOPHY OF PROGRESS
Higher Thinking for Developing Infinite Prosperity

THE ESSENCE OF BUDDHA
The Path to Enlightenment

THE CHALLENGE OF THE MIND
An Essential Guide to Buddha's Teachings:
Zen, Karma, and Enlightenment

THE CHALLENGE OF ENLIGHTENMENT
Realize Your Inner Potential

SOUTH KOREA'S CONSPIRACY

PRESIDENT PARK'S HIDDEN AGENDA TO UNITE WITH CHINA
ISBN: 978-1-937673-51-2
$14.95 (Paperback)

On June 27, 2013, South Korea's President Park Geun-hye and Chinese President Xi Jinping held summit talks in Beijing. At the meeting, President Park asked China's Xi Jinping to build a memorial of An Jung-geun, the man who in 1909 assassinated the first Prime Minister of Japan and the first Resident-General of Korea, Ito Hirobumi. In this spiritual interview, we begin by speaking with the spirit of An Jung-geun before moving on to a conversation with the guardian spirit of President Park, who forced herself into the interview out of fear that the interview will reveal the truth about him. Through these conversations, Master Ryuho Okawa tries to discover the facts about the assassination of Ito Hirobumi to determine whether An Jung-geun can justifiably be hailed as a hero. While South Koreans continue to accuse Japan of having wronged their nation, Master Okawa hopes that these interviews will provide a truthful understanding of the historical events between Japan and South Korea and help the international community understand the nature of true international justice.

UNMASKING BAN KI-MOON'S
BIASED STANCE

INVESTIGATING THE PARALYSIS OF THE UNITED NATIONS

ISBN: 978-1-937673-49-9
$14.95 (Paperback)

The world is currently facing many critical international issues that require resolution through strong leadership dedicated to the preservation of international peace and security. What are U.N. Secretary-General Ban Ki-moon's true thoughts on these pressing issues? What does he think about the disputes between Japan and South Korea over ownership of the Takeshima Islands, between Japan and China over ownership of the Senkaku Islands, and between Iran and Israel over nuclear weapons capability? Can we depend on him to successfully uphold the principle of impartiality in the United Nations's role of peacemaking? In this spiritual interview with the guardian spirit of Mr. Ban Ki-moon, Master Okawa reveals the U.N. Secretary-General's true character and true intentions regarding his important peacemaking responsibilities.

STEVE JOBS RETURNS
WITH HIS SECRETS
BE SIMPLE, BE CRAZY

ISBN: 978-1-937673-47-5
$19.95 (Paperback)

In this spiritual interview with Steve Jobs, conducted just three months after his death, Master Okawa offers us a chance to catch a glimpse into the mind of one of America's modern geniuses, whom President Barack Obama has described as one among the greatest American innovators. What was the aesthetic philosophy behind his passionate drive to create products that he described as "at the intersection of art and technology?" What were the secrets to his creativity and the successful sales of his products? As Master Okawa often says, and as this interview with the mind of one of the greatest modern innovators will show you, success is always in the way we think and in the substance of our goals and ideals.

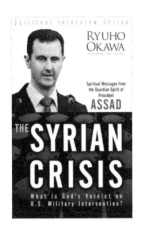

THE SYRIAN CRISIS

WHAT IS GOD'S VERDICT ON U.S. MILITARY INTERVENTION?

ISBN: 978-1-937673-44-4
$14.95 (Paperback)

Is there justice in a U.S. military intervention into the on-going Syrian crisis? What is God's perspective on the tragedy that is occurring in Syria? In *The Syrian Crisis: What Is God's Verdict on U.S. Military Intervention?* Master Ryuho Okawa conducts a spiritual interview with the guardian spirit of Bashar al-Assad. As this interview reveals, the Syrian dictator's true character is quite different from what we saw in the CBS interview. As the world braces for a possible world war, Master Ryuho Okawa provides us with a clear sense of where God's justice lies in this international crisis.

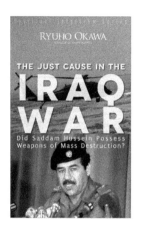

THE JUST CAUSE IN THE IRAQ WAR
DID SADDAM HUSSEIN POSSESS WEAPONS OF MASS DESTRUCTION?

ISBN: 978-1-937673-41-3
$14.95 (Paperback)

The Just Cause in the Iraq War: Did Saddam Hussein Possess Weapons of Mass Destruction? tackles one of the most controversial and pertinent issues in international politics today. Is President Obama correct that the Iraq War was an unjust war, as he claimed during the 2012 presidential race? Did Saddam Hussein truly have no weapons of mass destruction, or are those weapons still hidden in Iraq, somewhere beyond the reach of U.S. intelligence? In this book, you will discover that Saddam Hussein was also behind the planning of the 9/11 terrorist attacks and both he and Osama bin Laden are now in Hell. The knowledge this book provides will help each of us make the right decisions as we work together to create a peaceful international society.

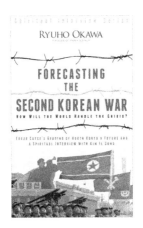

FORECASTING THE SECOND KOREAN WAR
HOW WILL THE WORLD HANDLE THE CRISIS?

ISBN: 978-1-937673-35-2
$14.95 (Paperback)

Forecasting the Second Korean War: How Will the World Handle the Crisis? forecasts a potential crisis that the United States, South Korea, and Japan may face. In part 1, Master Okawa draws on the help of Edgar Cayce to describe in detail the unfolding of a second Korean War that could begin in the summer of 2013. Part 2 of this book contains a spiritual interview with Kim Il Sung that reveals that he is spiritually guiding Kim Jong Un. Together, the two parts of this book reveal the shocking fact that the crisis on the Korean peninsula is only a small part of a larger and more global imperialistic scheme that is being masterminded by Xi Jinping, the president of China. You will discover who is truly behind the Islamist terrorist attacks against the United States.

MARGARET THATCHER'S
MIRACULOUS MESSAGE
AN INTERVIEW WITH THE IRON LADY
19 HOURS AFTER HER DEATH

ISBN: 978-1-937673-37-6
$14.95 (Paperback)

On April 9, 2013, just nineteen hours after Margaret Thatcher's death, Master Ryuho Okawa summoned her spirit to hold a miraculous spiritual interview with Europe's first female prime minister, famously known as the Iron Lady. In words marked by her signature clarity and determination, Margaret Thatcher provided valuable answers to essential and timely questions. Her answers will prove helpful not only to the United Kingdom, but also to the global economy and governments all over the world, including those of the United States and the European Union.

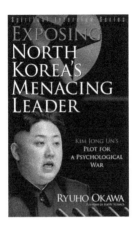

EXPOSING NORTH KOREA'S MENACING LEADER

KIM JONG UN'S PLOT FOR A PSYCHOLOGICAL WAR

ISBN: 978-1-937673-39-0
$14.95 (Paperback)

Exposing North Korea's Menacing Leader: Kim Jong Un's Plot for a Psychological War reveals the role that North Korea is playing in China's imperialistic strategy and the two nations' close ties with Iran. Together, China and Kim Jong Un—North Korea's supreme leader— are carrying out a psychological war that takes full advantage of the weaknesses of Japanese Prime Minister Abe and United States President Obama. Indeed, this interview with Kim Jong Un's guardian spirit reveals that Kim Jong Un was most likely behind the Boston marathon bombings that occurred on April 15, 2013.

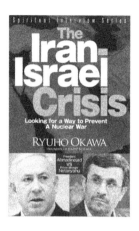

THE IRAN-ISRAEL CRISIS

LOOKING FOR A WAY TO PREVENT A NUCLEAR WAR

ISBN: 978-1-937673-26-0
$14.95 (Paperback)

Master Ryuho Okawa firmly believes that the power to create lasting global peace will come from embracing love and forgiveness beyond differences in religion. This set of spiritual interviews with the guardian spirits of Iran's President Mahmoud Ahmadinejad and Israel's Prime Minister Benjamin Netanyahu reveal their living counterparts' underlying ideas about each other's nations as arch enemies. You will discover hints to solving long-standing clashes between religions.

CHINA'S SECRET MILITARY BASES

A REMOTE-VIEWING INVESTIGATION
OF SUSPICIOUS SATELLITE IMAGES

ISBN: 978-1-937673-24-6
$14.95 (Paperback)

Master Okawa reveals China's versions of Area 51 from mysterious satellite photos that had aroused worldwide curiosity. Even American intelligence will be shocked to find out these truths about a hidden enormous missile-launching site full of nuclear warheads prepared to strike major cities around the world. This book is a must-read for anyone who wants to save the world from a full-out nuclear war.

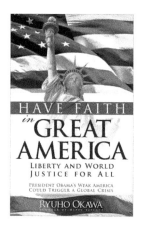

HAVE FAITH IN GREAT AMERICA
LIBERTY AND WORLD JUSTICE FOR ALL

ISBN: 978-1-937673-20-8
$14.95 (Paperback)

Have Faith in Great America: Liberty and World Justice for All is Master Ryuho Okawa's earnest message to the United States of America. The world's future depends on America's fulfillment of its long-held sacred mission of protecting the faith, liberty, and justice of people and nations around the world, and on the development of strong bonds between the United States and Japan.

CHINA'S HIDDEN AGENDA
THE MASTERMIND BEHIND THE ANTI-AMERICAN
AND ANTI-JAPANESE PROTESTS

ISBN: 978-1937673-18-5
$14.95 (Paperback)

"Anti-American demonstrations have been raging in over twenty Arab countries. The man pulling the strings behind all this is Xi Jinping."

—Master Ryuho Okawa

"I wanted to stir up the anti-American movement in the Arab world to make sure that the United States won't be able to attack Syria or Iran...I'm the mastermind behind the Muhammad video."

—Xi Jinping's Guardian Spirit

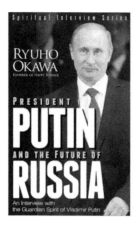

PRESIDENT PUTIN AND THE FUTURE OF RUSSIA

AN INTERVIEW WITH THE GUARDIAN SPIRIT
OF VLADIMIR PUTIN

ISBN: 978-1-937673-14-7
$14.95 (Paperback)

"I have no intention of fighting the United States. The Cold War is over... I have no intention of fighting the Americans... And I'm not friendly enough with China to think about joining them against the United States... I have given Russians religious freedom, which makes me very different from the Chinese."

—Putin's Guardian Spirit

2012 WILL THE WORLD
REALLY END?

MESSAGES FROM MONTEZUMA AND QUETZALCOATL

ISBN: 978-1-937673-07-9
$14.95 (Paperback)

Is the Mayan prophecy true? Will the world really come to an end in 2012? Master Ryuho Okawa, to help us prepare for that pivotal year, summoned two spirits involved in the Mayan prophecy: King Montezuma of the Aztec Empire and the Mesoamerican god, Quetzalcoatl. Through these conversations between Happy Science interviewers and these spirits speaking through Master Okawa, they disclosed valuable hints about the secrets behind the Mayan prophecy, as well as the meaning of the major political events of 2012.

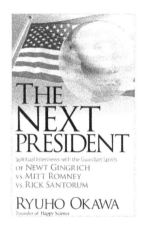

THE NEXT PRESIDENT

SPIRITUAL INTERVIEWS WITH THE GUARDIAN SPIRITS OF
NEWT GINGRICH VS. MITT ROMNEY VS. RICK SANTORUM

ISBN: 978-1-937673-12-3
$14.95 (Paperback)

This book reveals the honest and true intentions of the
three Republican leaders, Newt Gingrich, Mitt Romney,
and Rick Santorum, who were in a heated race for the GOP
presidential nomination when the interviews were held. In
three rare spiritual interviews by Happy Science, their guardian spirits speak through Master Ryuho Okawa to answer
questions about what they aim to accomplish if America
chooses them as the next President of the United States.

Lightning Source UK Ltd.
Milton Keynes UK
UKHW040945160223
417122UK00002B/422